## NAME

| BREWERY | TYPE / STYLE |
|---|---|
| ABV | IBU |
| ORIGIN | SAMPLED |

## SERVING TYPE

| CAN | BOTTLE | CASK | DRAFT | GROWLER | MIXED | OTHER |
|---|---|---|---|---|---|---|
| ☐ | ☐ | ☐ | ☐ | ☐ | ☐ | ☐ |

## BUBBLES & COLOR

HIGH

SPARKLING

MEDIUM

STILL

PALE AMBER
MEDIUM AMBER
DEEP AMBER
AMBER BROWN
BROWN
ERUBY BROWN

## FLAVOR WHEEL

CREAMY · SWEET · EARTHY · HERBAL · FLORAL · SPICY · BITTER · SOUR · HOPPY · MALTY · TOASTED · FRUITY · CARAMEL · COFFEE · NUTTY · DAIRY

## FINAL RATING

| APPEARANCE | ☆☆☆☆☆ |
|---|---|
| AROMA | ☆☆☆☆☆ |
| TASTE | ☆☆☆☆☆ |
| MOUTHFEEL | ☆☆☆☆☆ |
| OVERALL RATING | ☆☆☆☆☆ |

## ADDITIONAL NOTES

D1557500

## NAME

| BREWERY | TYPE / STYLE |
|---|---|
| ABV | IBU |
| ORIGIN | SAMPLED |

## SERVING TYPE

| CAN | BOTTLE | CASK | DRAFT | GROWLER | MIXED | OTHER |
|---|---|---|---|---|---|---|
| ☐ | ☐ | ☐ | ☐ | ☐ | ☐ | ☐ |

## BUBBLES & COLOR

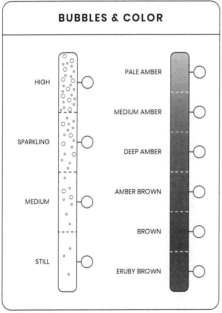

HIGH

SPARKLING

MEDIUM

STILL

PALE AMBER

MEDIUM AMBER

DEEP AMBER

AMBER BROWN

BROWN

ERUBY BROWN

## FLAVOR WHEEL

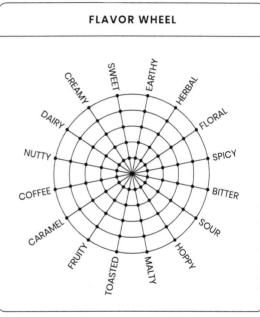

CREAMY · SWEET · EARTHY · HERBAL · FLORAL · SPICY · BITTER · SOUR · HOPPY · MALTY · TOASTED · FRUITY · CARAMEL · COFFEE · NUTTY · DAIRY

## FINAL RATING

| | |
|---|---|
| APPEARANCE | ☆☆☆☆☆ |
| AROMA | ☆☆☆☆☆ |
| TASTE | ☆☆☆☆☆ |
| MOUTHFEEL | ☆☆☆☆☆ |
| OVERALL RATING | ☆☆☆☆☆ |

## ADDITIONAL NOTES

## NAME

| BREWERY | TYPE / STYLE |
|---|---|
| ABV | IBU |
| ORIGIN | SAMPLED |

## SERVING TYPE

| CAN | BOTTLE | CASK | DRAFT | GROWLER | MIXED | OTHER |
|---|---|---|---|---|---|---|
| ☐ | ☐ | ☐ | ☐ | ☐ | ☐ | ☐ |

## BUBBLES & COLOR

HIGH

SPARKLING

MEDIUM

STILL

PALE AMBER

MEDIUM AMBER

DEEP AMBER

AMBER BROWN

BROWN

ERUBY BROWN

## FLAVOR WHEEL

CREAMY · SWEET · EARTHY · HERBAL · FLORAL · SPICY · BITTER · SOUR · HOPPY · MALTY · TOASTED · FRUITY · CARAMEL · COFFEE · NUTTY · DAIRY

## FINAL RATING

| APPEARANCE | ☆☆☆☆☆ |
|---|---|
| AROMA | ☆☆☆☆☆ |
| TASTE | ☆☆☆☆☆ |
| MOUTHFEEL | ☆☆☆☆☆ |
| OVERALL RATING | ☆☆☆☆☆ |

## ADDITIONAL NOTES

## NAME

| | | | |
|---|---|---|---|
| BREWERY | | TYPE / STYLE | |
| ABV | | IBU | |
| ORIGIN | | SAMPLED | |

## SERVING TYPE

| CAN | BOTTLE | CASK | DRAFT | GROWLER | MIXED | OTHER |
|---|---|---|---|---|---|---|
| ☐ | ☐ | ☐ | ☐ | ☐ | ☐ | ☐ |

## BUBBLES & COLOR

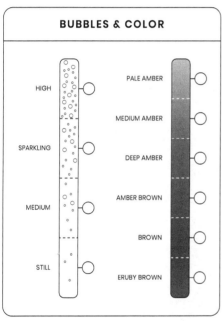

HIGH

SPARKLING

MEDIUM

STILL

PALE AMBER

MEDIUM AMBER

DEEP AMBER

AMBER BROWN

BROWN

ERUBY BROWN

## FLAVOR WHEEL

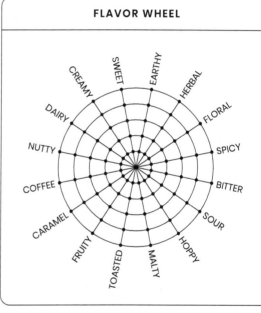

CREAMY · SWEET · EARTHY · HERBAL · FLORAL · SPICY · BITTER · SOUR · HOPPY · MALTY · TOASTED · FRUITY · CARAMEL · COFFEE · NUTTY · DAIRY

## FINAL RATING

| | | |
|---|---|---|
| APPEARANCE | ☆☆☆☆☆ |
| AROMA | ☆☆☆☆☆ |
| TASTE | ☆☆☆☆☆ |
| MOUTHFEEL | ☆☆☆☆☆ |
| OVERALL RATING | ☆☆☆☆☆ |

## ADDITIONAL NOTES

## NAME

## BREWERY

## ABV

## ORIGIN

## TYPE / STYLE

## IBU

## SAMPLED

---

## SERVING TYPE

| CAN | BOTTLE | CASK | DRAFT | GROWLER | MIXED | OTHER |
|-----|--------|------|-------|---------|-------|-------|
| ☐ | ☐ | ☐ | ☐ | ☐ | ☐ | ☐ |

---

## BUBBLES & COLOR

HIGH

SPARKLING

MEDIUM

STILL

PALE AMBER
MEDIUM AMBER
DEEP AMBER
AMBER BROWN
BROWN
ERUBY BROWN

## FLAVOR WHEEL

CREAMY · SWEET · EARTHY · HERBAL · FLORAL · SPICY · BITTER · SOUR · HOPPY · MALTY · TOASTED · FRUITY · CARAMEL · COFFEE · NUTTY · DAIRY

---

## FINAL RATING

| | | |
|---|---|---|
| APPEARANCE | ☆☆☆☆☆ |
| AROMA | ☆☆☆☆☆ |
| TASTE | ☆☆☆☆☆ |
| MOUTHFEEL | ☆☆☆☆☆ |
| OVERALL RATING | ☆☆☆☆☆ |

## ADDITIONAL NOTES

## NAME

| BREWERY | TYPE / STYLE |
|---|---|
| ABV | IBU |
| ORIGIN | SAMPLED |

## SERVING TYPE

| CAN | BOTTLE | CASK | DRAFT | GROWLER | MIXED | OTHER |
|---|---|---|---|---|---|---|
| ☐ | ☐ | ☐ | ☐ | ☐ | ☐ | ☐ |

## BUBBLES & COLOR

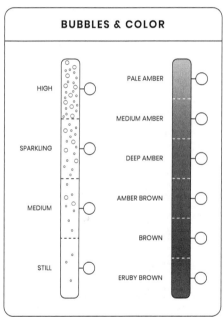

HIGH

SPARKLING

MEDIUM

STILL

PALE AMBER

MEDIUM AMBER

DEEP AMBER

AMBER BROWN

BROWN

ERUBY BROWN

## FLAVOR WHEEL

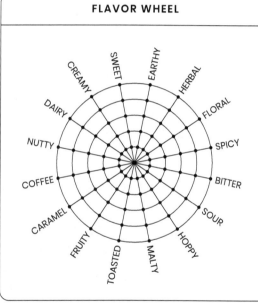

CREAMY · SWEET · EARTHY · HERBAL · FLORAL · SPICY · BITTER · SOUR · HOPPY · MALTY · TOASTED · FRUITY · CARAMEL · COFFEE · NUTTY · DAIRY

## FINAL RATING

| APPEARANCE | ☆☆☆☆☆ |
|---|---|
| AROMA | ☆☆☆☆☆ |
| TASTE | ☆☆☆☆☆ |
| MOUTHFEEL | ☆☆☆☆☆ |
| OVERALL RATING | ☆☆☆☆☆ |

## ADDITIONAL NOTES

| 🍺 NAME | |
|---|---|
| 🛢 BREWERY | 🍾 TYPE / STYLE |
| 🍶 ABV | 🌿 IBU |
| 🌍 ORIGIN | 📅 SAMPLED |

## SERVING TYPE

| CAN | BOTTLE | CASK | DRAFT | GROWLER | MIXED | OTHER |
|---|---|---|---|---|---|---|
| 🗃 | 🍾 | 🛢 | 🍺 | 🧃 | 🍹 | ⚗ |
| ☐ | ☐ | ☐ | ☐ | ☐ | ☐ | ☐ |

## BUBBLES & COLOR

HIGH

SPARKLING

MEDIUM

STILL

PALE AMBER

MEDIUM AMBER

DEEP AMBER

AMBER BROWN

BROWN

ERUBY BROWN

## FLAVOR WHEEL

CREAMY · SWEET · EARTHY · HERBAL · FLORAL · SPICY · BITTER · SOUR · HOPPY · MALTY · TOASTED · FRUITY · CARAMEL · COFFEE · NUTTY · DAIRY

## FINAL RATING

| 🍾 APPEARANCE | ☆☆☆☆☆ |
|---|---|
| 🌾 AROMA | ☆☆☆☆☆ |
| 🍺 TASTE | ☆☆☆☆☆ |
| 👄 MOUTHFEEL | ☆☆☆☆☆ |
| 🤲 OVERALL RATING | ☆☆☆☆☆ |

## ADDITIONAL NOTES

## NAME

| BREWERY | TYPE / STYLE |
|---|---|
| ABV | IBU |
| ORIGIN | SAMPLED |

## SERVING TYPE

| CAN | BOTTLE | CASK | DRAFT | GROWLER | MIXED | OTHER |
|---|---|---|---|---|---|---|
| ☐ | ☐ | ☐ | ☐ | ☐ | ☐ | ☐ |

## BUBBLES & COLOR

HIGH

SPARKLING

MEDIUM

STILL

PALE AMBER
MEDIUM AMBER
DEEP AMBER
AMBER BROWN
BROWN
ERUBY BROWN

## FLAVOR WHEEL

CREAMY · SWEET · EARTHY · HERBAL · FLORAL · SPICY · BITTER · SOUR · HOPPY · MALTY · TOASTED · FRUITY · CARAMEL · COFFEE · NUTTY · DAIRY

## FINAL RATING

| APPEARANCE | ☆☆☆☆☆ |
|---|---|
| AROMA | ☆☆☆☆☆ |
| TASTE | ☆☆☆☆☆ |
| MOUTHFEEL | ☆☆☆☆☆ |
| OVERALL RATING | ☆☆☆☆☆ |

## ADDITIONAL NOTES

## NAME

| BREWERY | TYPE / STYLE |
|---|---|
| ABV | IBU |
| ORIGIN | SAMPLED |

## SERVING TYPE

| CAN | BOTTLE | CASK | DRAFT | GROWLER | MIXED | OTHER |
|---|---|---|---|---|---|---|
| ☐ | ☐ | ☐ | ☐ | ☐ | ☐ | ☐ |

## BUBBLES & COLOR

HIGH ○

SPARKLING ○

MEDIUM ○

STILL ○

PALE AMBER ○

MEDIUM AMBER ○

DEEP AMBER ○

AMBER BROWN ○

BROWN ○

ERUBY BROWN ○

## FLAVOR WHEEL

CREAMY · SWEET · EARTHY · HERBAL · FLORAL · SPICY · BITTER · SOUR · HOPPY · MALTY · TOASTED · FRUITY · CARAMEL · COFFEE · NUTTY · DAIRY

## FINAL RATING

| APPEARANCE | ☆☆☆☆☆ |
|---|---|
| AROMA | ☆☆☆☆☆ |
| TASTE | ☆☆☆☆☆ |
| MOUTHFEEL | ☆☆☆☆☆ |
| OVERALL RATING | ☆☆☆☆☆ |

## ADDITIONAL NOTES

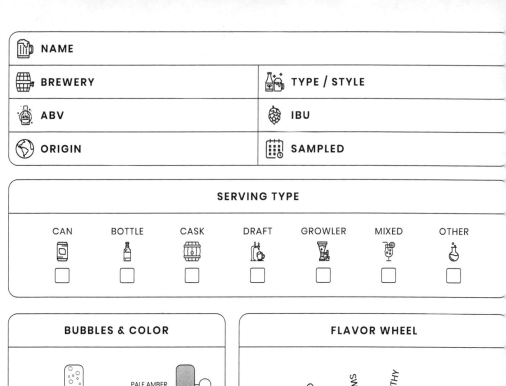

## NAME

## BREWERY

## TYPE / STYLE

## ABV

## IBU

## ORIGIN

## SAMPLED

## SERVING TYPE

| CAN | BOTTLE | CASK | DRAFT | GROWLER | MIXED | OTHER |
|-----|--------|------|-------|---------|-------|-------|
| ☐ | ☐ | ☐ | ☐ | ☐ | ☐ | ☐ |

## BUBBLES & COLOR

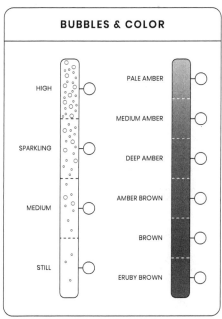

HIGH

SPARKLING

MEDIUM

STILL

PALE AMBER

MEDIUM AMBER

DEEP AMBER

AMBER BROWN

BROWN

ERUBY BROWN

## FLAVOR WHEEL

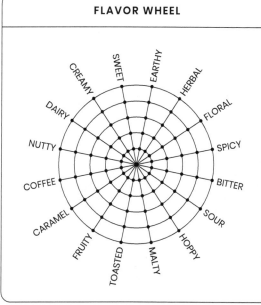

CREAMY · SWEET · EARTHY · HERBAL · FLORAL · DAIRY · SPICY · NUTTY · BITTER · COFFEE · SOUR · CARAMEL · HOPPY · FRUITY · TOASTED · MALTY

## FINAL RATING

| APPEARANCE | ☆☆☆☆☆ |
|------------|-------|
| AROMA | ☆☆☆☆☆ |
| TASTE | ☆☆☆☆☆ |
| MOUTHFEEL | ☆☆☆☆☆ |
| OVERALL RATING | ☆☆☆☆☆ |

## ADDITIONAL NOTES

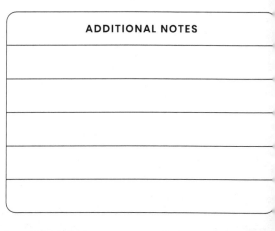

## NAME

## BREWERY | TYPE / STYLE

## ABV | IBU

## ORIGIN | SAMPLED

## SERVING TYPE

| CAN | BOTTLE | CASK | DRAFT | GROWLER | MIXED | OTHER |
|-----|--------|------|-------|---------|-------|-------|
| ☐ | ☐ | ☐ | ☐ | ☐ | ☐ | ☐ |

## BUBBLES & COLOR

HIGH

SPARKLING

MEDIUM

STILL

PALE AMBER

MEDIUM AMBER

DEEP AMBER

AMBER BROWN

BROWN

ERUBY BROWN

## FLAVOR WHEEL

CREAMY
SWEET
EARTHY
HERBAL
DAIRY
FLORAL
NUTTY
SPICY
COFFEE
BITTER
CARAMEL
SOUR
FRUITY
HOPPY
TOASTED
MALTY

## FINAL RATING

APPEARANCE ☆☆☆☆☆

AROMA ☆☆☆☆☆

TASTE ☆☆☆☆☆

MOUTHFEEL ☆☆☆☆☆

OVERALL RATING ☆☆☆☆☆

## ADDITIONAL NOTES

## NAME

| | |
|---|---|
| **BREWERY** | **TYPE / STYLE** |
| **ABV** | **IBU** |
| **ORIGIN** | **SAMPLED** |

## SERVING TYPE

| CAN | BOTTLE | CASK | DRAFT | GROWLER | MIXED | OTHER |
|---|---|---|---|---|---|---|
| ☐ | ☐ | ☐ | ☐ | ☐ | ☐ | ☐ |

## BUBBLES & COLOR

HIGH

SPARKLING

MEDIUM

STILL

PALE AMBER

MEDIUM AMBER

DEEP AMBER

AMBER BROWN

BROWN

ERUBY BROWN

## FLAVOR WHEEL

CREAMY · SWEET · EARTHY · HERBAL · FLORAL · SPICY · BITTER · SOUR · HOPPY · MALTY · TOASTED · FRUITY · CARAMEL · COFFEE · NUTTY · DAIRY

## FINAL RATING

APPEARANCE ☆☆☆☆☆

AROMA ☆☆☆☆☆

TASTE ☆☆☆☆☆

MOUTHFEEL ☆☆☆☆☆

OVERALL RATING ☆☆☆☆☆

## ADDITIONAL NOTES

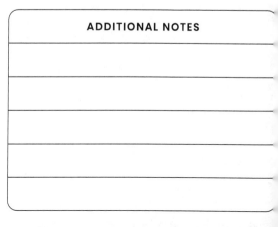

## NAME

| | | | |
|---|---|---|---|
| BREWERY | | TYPE / STYLE | |
| ABV | | IBU | |
| ORIGIN | | SAMPLED | |

## SERVING TYPE

| CAN | BOTTLE | CASK | DRAFT | GROWLER | MIXED | OTHER |
|---|---|---|---|---|---|---|
| ☐ | ☐ | ☐ | ☐ | ☐ | ☐ | ☐ |

## BUBBLES & COLOR

HIGH

SPARKLING

MEDIUM

STILL

PALE AMBER

MEDIUM AMBER

DEEP AMBER

AMBER BROWN

BROWN

ERUBY BROWN

## FLAVOR WHEEL

SWEET · EARTHY · HERBAL · FLORAL · SPICY · BITTER · SOUR · HOPPY · MALTY · TOASTED · FRUITY · CARAMEL · COFFEE · NUTTY · DAIRY · CREAMY

## FINAL RATING

| APPEARANCE | ☆☆☆☆☆ |
|---|---|
| AROMA | ☆☆☆☆☆ |
| TASTE | ☆☆☆☆☆ |
| MOUTHFEEL | ☆☆☆☆☆ |
| OVERALL RATING | ☆☆☆☆☆ |

## ADDITIONAL NOTES

| 🍺 NAME | |
|---|---|
| 🛢️ BREWERY | 🍾 TYPE / STYLE |
| 🥃 ABV | 🌰 IBU |
| 🌍 ORIGIN | 📅 SAMPLED |

## SERVING TYPE

| CAN | BOTTLE | CASK | DRAFT | GROWLER | MIXED | OTHER |
|---|---|---|---|---|---|---|
| 📦 | 🍾 | 🛢️ | 🍺 | 🥤 | 🍹 | ⚗️ |
| ☐ | ☐ | ☐ | ☐ | ☐ | ☐ | ☐ |

## BUBBLES & COLOR

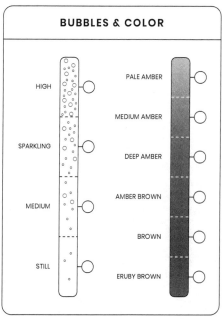

HIGH

SPARKLING

MEDIUM

STILL

PALE AMBER

MEDIUM AMBER

DEEP AMBER

AMBER BROWN

BROWN

ERUBY BROWN

## FLAVOR WHEEL

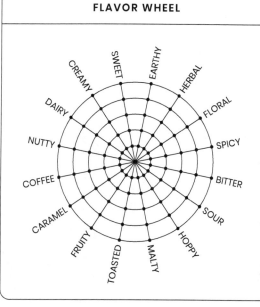

CREAMY · SWEET · EARTHY · HERBAL · DAIRY · FLORAL · NUTTY · SPICY · COFFEE · BITTER · CARAMEL · SOUR · FRUITY · TOASTED · MALTY · HOPPY

## FINAL RATING

| | | |
|---|---|---|
| 🍾 APPEARANCE | ☆☆☆☆☆ |
| 🌾 AROMA | ☆☆☆☆☆ |
| 🍺 TASTE | ☆☆☆☆☆ |
| 👄 MOUTHFEEL | ☆☆☆☆☆ |
| 🤲 OVERALL RATING | ☆☆☆☆☆ |

## ADDITIONAL NOTES

| NAME | |
|------|--|
| BREWERY | TYPE / STYLE |
| ABV | IBU |
| ORIGIN | SAMPLED |

## SERVING TYPE

| CAN | BOTTLE | CASK | DRAFT | GROWLER | MIXED | OTHER |
|-----|--------|------|-------|---------|-------|-------|
| ☐ | ☐ | ☐ | ☐ | ☐ | ☐ | ☐ |

## BUBBLES & COLOR

HIGH

SPARKLING

MEDIUM

STILL

PALE AMBER

MEDIUM AMBER

DEEP AMBER

AMBER BROWN

BROWN

ERUBY BROWN

## FLAVOR WHEEL

CREAMY · SWEET · EARTHY · HERBAL · FLORAL · SPICY · BITTER · SOUR · HOPPY · MALTY · TOASTED · FRUITY · CARAMEL · COFFEE · NUTTY · DAIRY

## FINAL RATING

| | | |
|--|--|--|
| APPEARANCE | ☆☆☆☆☆ |
| AROMA | ☆☆☆☆☆ |
| TASTE | ☆☆☆☆☆ |
| MOUTHFEEL | ☆☆☆☆☆ |
| OVERALL RATING | ☆☆☆☆☆ |

## ADDITIONAL NOTES

## NAME

| BREWERY | TYPE / STYLE |
|---|---|
| ABV | IBU |
| ORIGIN | SAMPLED |

## SERVING TYPE

| CAN | BOTTLE | CASK | DRAFT | GROWLER | MIXED | OTHER |
|---|---|---|---|---|---|---|
| ☐ | ☐ | ☐ | ☐ | ☐ | ☐ | ☐ |

## BUBBLES & COLOR

HIGH

SPARKLING

MEDIUM

STILL

PALE AMBER

MEDIUM AMBER

DEEP AMBER

AMBER BROWN

BROWN

ERUBY BROWN

## FLAVOR WHEEL

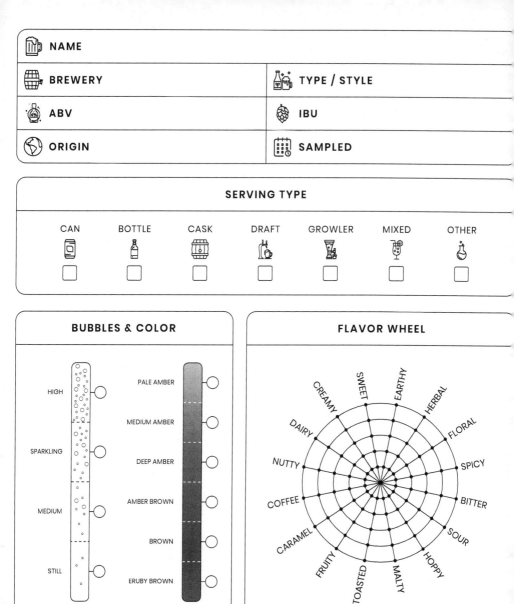

CREAMY · SWEET · EARTHY · HERBAL · FLORAL · SPICY · BITTER · SOUR · HOPPY · MALTY · TOASTED · FRUITY · CARAMEL · COFFEE · NUTTY · DAIRY

## FINAL RATING

| APPEARANCE | ☆☆☆☆☆ |
|---|---|
| AROMA | ☆☆☆☆☆ |
| TASTE | ☆☆☆☆☆ |
| MOUTHFEEL | ☆☆☆☆☆ |
| OVERALL RATING | ☆☆☆☆☆ |

## ADDITIONAL NOTES

## NAME

| | |
|---|---|
| **BREWERY** | **TYPE / STYLE** |
| **ABV** | **IBU** |
| **ORIGIN** | **SAMPLED** |

## SERVING TYPE

| CAN | BOTTLE | CASK | DRAFT | GROWLER | MIXED | OTHER |
|---|---|---|---|---|---|---|
| ☐ | ☐ | ☐ | ☐ | ☐ | ☐ | ☐ |

## BUBBLES & COLOR

HIGH

SPARKLING

MEDIUM

STILL

PALE AMBER
MEDIUM AMBER
DEEP AMBER
AMBER BROWN
BROWN
ERUBY BROWN

## FLAVOR WHEEL

CREAMY · SWEET · EARTHY · HERBAL · FLORAL · SPICY · BITTER · SOUR · HOPPY · MALTY · TOASTED · FRUITY · CARAMEL · COFFEE · NUTTY · DAIRY

## FINAL RATING

| | | |
|---|---|---|
| APPEARANCE | ☆☆☆☆☆ |
| AROMA | ☆☆☆☆☆ |
| TASTE | ☆☆☆☆☆ |
| MOUTHFEEL | ☆☆☆☆☆ |
| OVERALL RATING | ☆☆☆☆☆ |

## ADDITIONAL NOTES

| 🍺 NAME | |
|---|---|
| 🛢️ BREWERY | 🍾 TYPE / STYLE |
| 🥃 ABV | 🌿 IBU |
| 🌍 ORIGIN | 📅 SAMPLED |

## SERVING TYPE

| CAN | BOTTLE | CASK | DRAFT | GROWLER | MIXED | OTHER |
|---|---|---|---|---|---|---|
| 🥫 ☐ | 🍾 ☐ | 🛢️ ☐ | 🍺 ☐ | 🧃 ☐ | 🍹 ☐ | ⚗️ ☐ |

## BUBBLES & COLOR

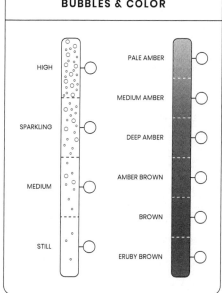

HIGH

SPARKLING

MEDIUM

STILL

PALE AMBER

MEDIUM AMBER

DEEP AMBER

AMBER BROWN

BROWN

ERUBY BROWN

## FLAVOR WHEEL

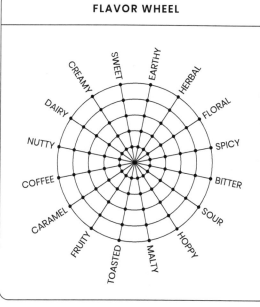

CREAMY · SWEET · EARTHY · HERBAL · DAIRY · FLORAL · NUTTY · SPICY · COFFEE · BITTER · CARAMEL · SOUR · FRUITY · HOPPY · TOASTED · MALTY

## FINAL RATING

| | | |
|---|---|---|
| 🍾 APPEARANCE | ☆☆☆☆☆ |
| 🌾 AROMA | ☆☆☆☆☆ |
| 🍺 TASTE | ☆☆☆☆☆ |
| 👄 MOUTHFEEL | ☆☆☆☆☆ |
| 🖐️ OVERALL RATING | ☆☆☆☆☆ |

## ADDITIONAL NOTES

## NAME

| BREWERY | TYPE / STYLE |
|---|---|
| ABV | IBU |
| ORIGIN | SAMPLED |

## SERVING TYPE

| CAN | BOTTLE | CASK | DRAFT | GROWLER | MIXED | OTHER |
|---|---|---|---|---|---|---|
| ☐ | ☐ | ☐ | ☐ | ☐ | ☐ | ☐ |

## BUBBLES & COLOR

HIGH

SPARKLING

MEDIUM

STILL

PALE AMBER

MEDIUM AMBER

DEEP AMBER

AMBER BROWN

BROWN

ERUBY BROWN

## FLAVOR WHEEL

SWEET
CREAMY
EARTHY
DAIRY
HERBAL
NUTTY
FLORAL
COFFEE
SPICY
CARAMEL
BITTER
FRUITY
SOUR
TOASTED
HOPPY
MALTY

## FINAL RATING

| APPEARANCE | ☆☆☆☆☆ |
|---|---|
| AROMA | ☆☆☆☆☆ |
| TASTE | ☆☆☆☆☆ |
| MOUTHFEEL | ☆☆☆☆☆ |
| OVERALL RATING | ☆☆☆☆☆ |

## ADDITIONAL NOTES

| 🍺 **NAME** | |
|---|---|
| 🛢 **BREWERY** | 🍾 **TYPE / STYLE** |
| 🥃 **ABV** | 🌺 **IBU** |
| 🌍 **ORIGIN** | 📅 **SAMPLED** |

## SERVING TYPE

| CAN | BOTTLE | CASK | DRAFT | GROWLER | MIXED | OTHER |
|---|---|---|---|---|---|---|
| 📱 | 🍾 | 🛢 | 🍺 | 🥤 | 🍹 | ⚗️ |
| ☐ | ☐ | ☐ | ☐ | ☐ | ☐ | ☐ |

## BUBBLES & COLOR

HIGH

SPARKLING

MEDIUM

STILL

PALE AMBER

MEDIUM AMBER

DEEP AMBER

AMBER BROWN

BROWN

ERUBY BROWN

## FLAVOR WHEEL

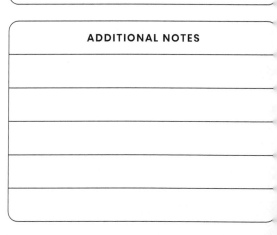

CREAMY · SWEET · EARTHY · HERBAL · DAIRY · FLORAL · NUTTY · SPICY · COFFEE · BITTER · CARAMEL · SOUR · FRUITY · HOPPY · TOASTED · MALTY

## FINAL RATING

| | | |
|---|---|---|
| 🍾 | APPEARANCE | ☆☆☆☆☆ |
| 🌾 | AROMA | ☆☆☆☆☆ |
| 🍺 | TASTE | ☆☆☆☆☆ |
| 👄 | MOUTHFEEL | ☆☆☆☆☆ |
| 🤚 | OVERALL RATING | ☆☆☆☆☆ |

## ADDITIONAL NOTES

## NAME

## BREWERY

## TYPE / STYLE

## ABV

## IBU

## ORIGIN

## SAMPLED

## SERVING TYPE

| CAN | BOTTLE | CASK | DRAFT | GROWLER | MIXED | OTHER |
|-----|--------|------|-------|---------|-------|-------|
| ☐ | ☐ | ☐ | ☐ | ☐ | ☐ | ☐ |

## BUBBLES & COLOR

HIGH

SPARKLING

MEDIUM

STILL

PALE AMBER

MEDIUM AMBER

DEEP AMBER

AMBER BROWN

BROWN

ERUBY BROWN

## FLAVOR WHEEL

CREAMY
SWEET
EARTHY
HERBAL
DAIRY
FLORAL
NUTTY
SPICY
COFFEE
BITTER
CARAMEL
SOUR
FRUITY
HOPPY
TOASTED
MALTY

## FINAL RATING

| APPEARANCE | ☆☆☆☆☆ |
|------------|-------|
| AROMA | ☆☆☆☆☆ |
| TASTE | ☆☆☆☆☆ |
| MOUTHFEEL | ☆☆☆☆☆ |
| OVERALL RATING | ☆☆☆☆☆ |

## ADDITIONAL NOTES

## NAME

| BREWERY | TYPE / STYLE |
|---|---|
| ABV | IBU |
| ORIGIN | SAMPLED |

## SERVING TYPE

| CAN | BOTTLE | CASK | DRAFT | GROWLER | MIXED | OTHER |
|---|---|---|---|---|---|---|
| ☐ | ☐ | ☐ | ☐ | ☐ | ☐ | ☐ |

## BUBBLES & COLOR

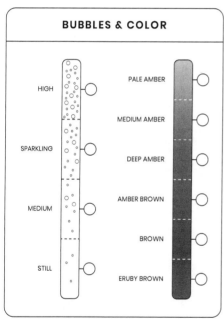

HIGH

SPARKLING

MEDIUM

STILL

PALE AMBER

MEDIUM AMBER

DEEP AMBER

AMBER BROWN

BROWN

ERUBY BROWN

## FLAVOR WHEEL

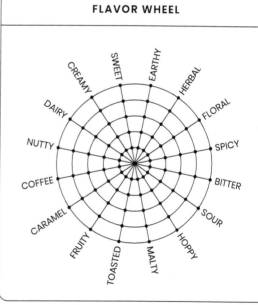

## FINAL RATING

| APPEARANCE | ☆☆☆☆☆ |
|---|---|
| AROMA | ☆☆☆☆☆ |
| TASTE | ☆☆☆☆☆ |
| MOUTHFEEL | ☆☆☆☆☆ |
| OVERALL RATING | ☆☆☆☆☆ |

## ADDITIONAL NOTES

| 🍺 NAME | |
|---|---|
| 🛢️ BREWERY | 🍶 TYPE / STYLE |
| 🍾 ABV | 🌿 IBU |
| 🌍 ORIGIN | 📅 SAMPLED |

## SERVING TYPE

| CAN | BOTTLE | CASK | DRAFT | GROWLER | MIXED | OTHER |
|---|---|---|---|---|---|---|
| ☐ | ☐ | ☐ | ☐ | ☐ | ☐ | ☐ |

## BUBBLES & COLOR

HIGH ◯

SPARKLING ◯

MEDIUM ◯

STILL ◯

PALE AMBER ◯

MEDIUM AMBER ◯

DEEP AMBER ◯

AMBER BROWN ◯

BROWN ◯

ERUBY BROWN ◯

## FLAVOR WHEEL

CREAMY · SWEET · EARTHY · HERBAL · FLORAL · SPICY · BITTER · SOUR · HOPPY · MALTY · TOASTED · FRUITY · CARAMEL · COFFEE · NUTTY · DAIRY

## FINAL RATING

| 🍾 APPEARANCE | ☆☆☆☆☆ |
|---|---|
| 🌾 AROMA | ☆☆☆☆☆ |
| 🍺 TASTE | ☆☆☆☆☆ |
| 👄 MOUTHFEEL | ☆☆☆☆☆ |
| 🖐️ OVERALL RATING | ☆☆☆☆☆ |

## ADDITIONAL NOTES

## NAME

| BREWERY | TYPE / STYLE |
|---|---|
| ABV | IBU |
| ORIGIN | SAMPLED |

## SERVING TYPE

| CAN | BOTTLE | CASK | DRAFT | GROWLER | MIXED | OTHER |
|---|---|---|---|---|---|---|
| ☐ | ☐ | ☐ | ☐ | ☐ | ☐ | ☐ |

## BUBBLES & COLOR

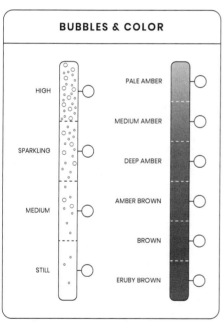

HIGH

SPARKLING

MEDIUM

STILL

PALE AMBER

MEDIUM AMBER

DEEP AMBER

AMBER BROWN

BROWN

ERUBY BROWN

## FLAVOR WHEEL

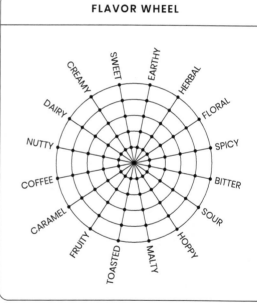

CREAMY · SWEET · EARTHY · HERBAL · DAIRY · FLORAL · NUTTY · SPICY · COFFEE · BITTER · CARAMEL · SOUR · FRUITY · HOPPY · TOASTED · MALTY

## FINAL RATING

| APPEARANCE | ☆☆☆☆☆ |
|---|---|
| AROMA | ☆☆☆☆☆ |
| TASTE | ☆☆☆☆☆ |
| MOUTHFEEL | ☆☆☆☆☆ |
| OVERALL RATING | ☆☆☆☆☆ |

## ADDITIONAL NOTES

## NAME

| | |
|---|---|
| **BREWERY** | **TYPE / STYLE** |
| **ABV** | **IBU** |
| **ORIGIN** | **SAMPLED** |

## SERVING TYPE

| CAN | BOTTLE | CASK | DRAFT | GROWLER | MIXED | OTHER |
|---|---|---|---|---|---|---|
| ☐ | ☐ | ☐ | ☐ | ☐ | ☐ | ☐ |

## BUBBLES & COLOR

HIGH

SPARKLING

MEDIUM

STILL

PALE AMBER

MEDIUM AMBER

DEEP AMBER

AMBER BROWN

BROWN

ERUBY BROWN

## FLAVOR WHEEL

CREAMY · SWEET · EARTHY · HERBAL · FLORAL · SPICY · BITTER · SOUR · HOPPY · MALTY · TOASTED · FRUITY · CARAMEL · COFFEE · NUTTY · DAIRY

## FINAL RATING

| | | |
|---|---|---|
| APPEARANCE | ☆☆☆☆☆ |
| AROMA | ☆☆☆☆☆ |
| TASTE | ☆☆☆☆☆ |
| MOUTHFEEL | ☆☆☆☆☆ |
| OVERALL RATING | ☆☆☆☆☆ |

## ADDITIONAL NOTES

# NAME

| BREWERY | TYPE / STYLE |
|---|---|
| ABV | IBU |
| ORIGIN | SAMPLED |

## SERVING TYPE

| CAN | BOTTLE | CASK | DRAFT | GROWLER | MIXED | OTHER |
|---|---|---|---|---|---|---|
| ☐ | ☐ | ☐ | ☐ | ☐ | ☐ | ☐ |

## BUBBLES & COLOR

HIGH

SPARKLING

MEDIUM

STILL

PALE AMBER

MEDIUM AMBER

DEEP AMBER

AMBER BROWN

BROWN

ERUBY BROWN

## FLAVOR WHEEL

CREAMY
SWEET
EARTHY
HERBAL
DAIRY
FLORAL
NUTTY
SPICY
COFFEE
BITTER
CARAMEL
SOUR
FRUITY
HOPPY
TOASTED
MALTY

## FINAL RATING

APPEARANCE ☆☆☆☆☆

AROMA ☆☆☆☆☆

TASTE ☆☆☆☆☆

MOUTHFEEL ☆☆☆☆☆

OVERALL RATING ☆☆☆☆☆

## ADDITIONAL NOTES

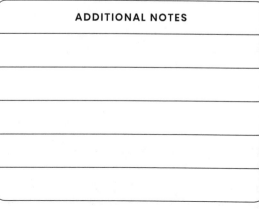

# NAME

| BREWERY | TYPE / STYLE |
| --- | --- |
| ABV | IBU |
| ORIGIN | SAMPLED |

## SERVING TYPE

| CAN | BOTTLE | CASK | DRAFT | GROWLER | MIXED | OTHER |
| --- | --- | --- | --- | --- | --- | --- |
| ☐ | ☐ | ☐ | ☐ | ☐ | ☐ | ☐ |

## BUBBLES & COLOR

HIGH

SPARKLING

MEDIUM

STILL

PALE AMBER
MEDIUM AMBER
DEEP AMBER
AMBER BROWN
BROWN
ERUBY BROWN

## FLAVOR WHEEL

CREAMY · SWEET · EARTHY · HERBAL · FLORAL · SPICY · BITTER · SOUR · HOPPY · MALTY · TOASTED · FRUITY · CARAMEL · COFFEE · NUTTY · DAIRY

## FINAL RATING

| APPEARANCE | ☆☆☆☆☆ |
| --- | --- |
| AROMA | ☆☆☆☆☆ |
| TASTE | ☆☆☆☆☆ |
| MOUTHFEEL | ☆☆☆☆☆ |
| OVERALL RATING | ☆☆☆☆☆ |

## ADDITIONAL NOTES

## NAME

| BREWERY | TYPE / STYLE |
|---|---|
| ABV | IBU |
| ORIGIN | SAMPLED |

## SERVING TYPE

| CAN | BOTTLE | CASK | DRAFT | GROWLER | MIXED | OTHER |
|---|---|---|---|---|---|---|
| ☐ | ☐ | ☐ | ☐ | ☐ | ☐ | ☐ |

## BUBBLES & COLOR

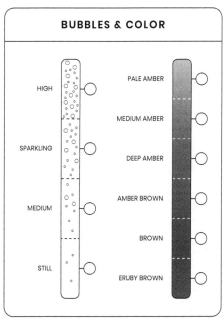

HIGH

SPARKLING

MEDIUM

STILL

PALE AMBER

MEDIUM AMBER

DEEP AMBER

AMBER BROWN

BROWN

ERUBY BROWN

## FLAVOR WHEEL

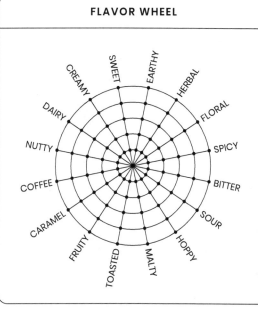

CREAMY · SWEET · EARTHY · HERBAL · DAIRY · FLORAL · NUTTY · SPICY · COFFEE · BITTER · CARAMEL · SOUR · FRUITY · HOPPY · TOASTED · MALTY

## FINAL RATING

| APPEARANCE | ☆☆☆☆☆ |
|---|---|
| AROMA | ☆☆☆☆☆ |
| TASTE | ☆☆☆☆☆ |
| MOUTHFEEL | ☆☆☆☆☆ |
| OVERALL RATING | ☆☆☆☆☆ |

## ADDITIONAL NOTES

# NAME

| BREWERY | TYPE / STYLE |
|---|---|
| ABV | IBU |
| ORIGIN | SAMPLED |

## SERVING TYPE

| CAN | BOTTLE | CASK | DRAFT | GROWLER | MIXED | OTHER |
|---|---|---|---|---|---|---|
| ☐ | ☐ | ☐ | ☐ | ☐ | ☐ | ☐ |

## BUBBLES & COLOR

HIGH

SPARKLING

MEDIUM

STILL

PALE AMBER ◯

MEDIUM AMBER ◯

DEEP AMBER ◯

AMBER BROWN ◯

BROWN ◯

ERUBY BROWN ◯

## FLAVOR WHEEL

CREAMY — SWEET — EARTHY — HERBAL — FLORAL — SPICY — BITTER — SOUR — HOPPY — MALTY — TOASTED — FRUITY — CARAMEL — COFFEE — NUTTY — DAIRY

## FINAL RATING

| APPEARANCE | ☆☆☆☆☆ |
|---|---|
| AROMA | ☆☆☆☆☆ |
| TASTE | ☆☆☆☆☆ |
| MOUTHFEEL | ☆☆☆☆☆ |
| OVERALL RATING | ☆☆☆☆☆ |

## ADDITIONAL NOTES

| 🍺 NAME | |
|---|---|
| 🛢 BREWERY | 🍾 TYPE / STYLE |
| 🍶 ABV | 🌿 IBU |
| 🌍 ORIGIN | 📅 SAMPLED |

## SERVING TYPE

| CAN | BOTTLE | CASK | DRAFT | GROWLER | MIXED | OTHER |
|---|---|---|---|---|---|---|
| 🥫 | 🍾 | 🛢 | 🍺 | 🧃 | 🍹 | ⚗ |
| ☐ | ☐ | ☐ | ☐ | ☐ | ☐ | ☐ |

## BUBBLES & COLOR

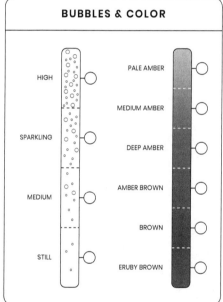

HIGH

SPARKLING

MEDIUM

STILL

PALE AMBER
MEDIUM AMBER
DEEP AMBER
AMBER BROWN
BROWN
ERUBY BROWN

## FLAVOR WHEEL

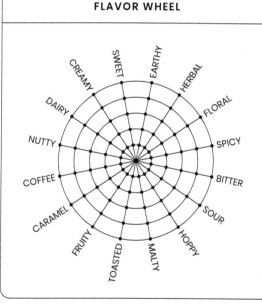

CREAMY · SWEET · EARTHY · HERBAL · DAIRY · FLORAL · NUTTY · SPICY · COFFEE · BITTER · CARAMEL · SOUR · FRUITY · TOASTED · MALTY · HOPPY

## FINAL RATING

| | | |
|---|---|---|
| 🍾 APPEARANCE | ☆☆☆☆☆ |
| 🌾 AROMA | ☆☆☆☆☆ |
| 🍺 TASTE | ☆☆☆☆☆ |
| 👄 MOUTHFEEL | ☆☆☆☆☆ |
| ✍ OVERALL RATING | ☆☆☆☆☆ |

## ADDITIONAL NOTES

## NAME

| | | | |
|---|---|---|---|
| BREWERY | | TYPE / STYLE | |
| ABV | | IBU | |
| ORIGIN | | SAMPLED | |

## SERVING TYPE

| CAN | BOTTLE | CASK | DRAFT | GROWLER | MIXED | OTHER |
|---|---|---|---|---|---|---|
| ☐ | ☐ | ☐ | ☐ | ☐ | ☐ | ☐ |

## BUBBLES & COLOR

HIGH

SPARKLING

MEDIUM

STILL

PALE AMBER
MEDIUM AMBER
DEEP AMBER
AMBER BROWN
BROWN
ERUBY BROWN

## FLAVOR WHEEL

CREAMY
SWEET
EARTHY
HERBAL
DAIRY
FLORAL
NUTTY
SPICY
COFFEE
BITTER
CARAMEL
SOUR
FRUITY
HOPPY
TOASTED
MALTY

## FINAL RATING

| APPEARANCE | ☆☆☆☆☆ |
|---|---|
| AROMA | ☆☆☆☆☆ |
| TASTE | ☆☆☆☆☆ |
| MOUTHFEEL | ☆☆☆☆☆ |
| OVERALL RATING | ☆☆☆☆☆ |

## ADDITIONAL NOTES

## NAME

| BREWERY | TYPE / STYLE |
|---|---|
| ABV | IBU |
| ORIGIN | SAMPLED |

## SERVING TYPE

| CAN | BOTTLE | CASK | DRAFT | GROWLER | MIXED | OTHER |
|---|---|---|---|---|---|---|
| ☐ | ☐ | ☐ | ☐ | ☐ | ☐ | ☐ |

## BUBBLES & COLOR

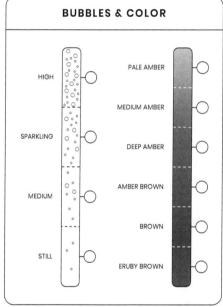

HIGH

SPARKLING

MEDIUM

STILL

PALE AMBER

MEDIUM AMBER

DEEP AMBER

AMBER BROWN

BROWN

ERUBY BROWN

## FLAVOR WHEEL

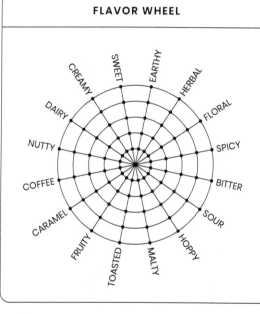

CREAMY · SWEET · EARTHY · HERBAL · DAIRY · FLORAL · NUTTY · SPICY · COFFEE · BITTER · CARAMEL · SOUR · FRUITY · HOPPY · TOASTED · MALTY

## FINAL RATING

| APPEARANCE | ☆☆☆☆☆ |
|---|---|
| AROMA | ☆☆☆☆☆ |
| TASTE | ☆☆☆☆☆ |
| MOUTHFEEL | ☆☆☆☆☆ |
| OVERALL RATING | ☆☆☆☆☆ |

## ADDITIONAL NOTES

| 🍺 NAME | |
|---|---|
| 🛢 BREWERY | 🍾 TYPE / STYLE |
| 🍶 ABV | 🌿 IBU |
| 🌍 ORIGIN | 📅 SAMPLED |

## SERVING TYPE

| CAN | BOTTLE | CASK | DRAFT | GROWLER | MIXED | OTHER |
|---|---|---|---|---|---|---|
| 🥫 | 🍾 | 🛢 | 🍺 | 🥤 | 🍹 | ⚗ |
| ☐ | ☐ | ☐ | ☐ | ☐ | ☐ | ☐ |

## BUBBLES & COLOR

HIGH

SPARKLING

MEDIUM

STILL

PALE AMBER ○
MEDIUM AMBER ○
DEEP AMBER ○
AMBER BROWN ○
BROWN ○
ERUBY BROWN ○

## FLAVOR WHEEL

CREAMY · SWEET · EARTHY · HERBAL · FLORAL · SPICY · BITTER · SOUR · HOPPY · MALTY · TOASTED · FRUITY · CARAMEL · COFFEE · NUTTY · DAIRY

## FINAL RATING

| 🍾 APPEARANCE | ☆☆☆☆☆ |
|---|---|
| 🌾 AROMA | ☆☆☆☆☆ |
| 🍺 TASTE | ☆☆☆☆☆ |
| 👄 MOUTHFEEL | ☆☆☆☆☆ |
| 🤲 OVERALL RATING | ☆☆☆☆☆ |

## ADDITIONAL NOTES

| 🍺 **NAME** | |
|---|---|
| 🛢️ **BREWERY** | 🍾 **TYPE / STYLE** |
| 🥃 **ABV** | 🌿 **IBU** |
| 🌍 **ORIGIN** | 📅 **SAMPLED** |

## SERVING TYPE

| CAN | BOTTLE | CASK | DRAFT | GROWLER | MIXED | OTHER |
|---|---|---|---|---|---|---|
| 🗄️ | 🍾 | 🛢️ | 🍺 | 🥤 | 🍹 | ⚗️ |
| ☐ | ☐ | ☐ | ☐ | ☐ | ☐ | ☐ |

## BUBBLES & COLOR

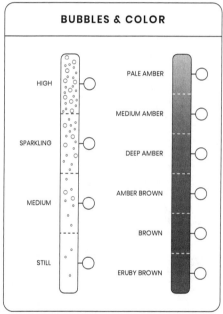

HIGH

SPARKLING

MEDIUM

STILL

PALE AMBER ○

MEDIUM AMBER ○

DEEP AMBER ○

AMBER BROWN ○

BROWN ○

ERUBY BROWN ○

## FLAVOR WHEEL

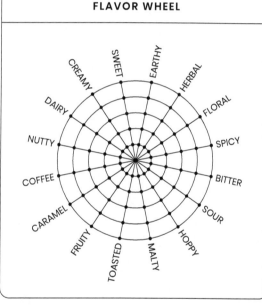

CREAMY · SWEET · EARTHY · HERBAL · DAIRY · FLORAL · NUTTY · SPICY · COFFEE · BITTER · CARAMEL · SOUR · FRUITY · HOPPY · TOASTED · MALTY

## FINAL RATING

| 🍾 APPEARANCE | ☆☆☆☆☆ |
|---|---|
| 🌾 AROMA | ☆☆☆☆☆ |
| 🍺 TASTE | ☆☆☆☆☆ |
| 👄 MOUTHFEEL | ☆☆☆☆☆ |
| ✍️ OVERALL RATING | ☆☆☆☆☆ |

## ADDITIONAL NOTES

## NAME

| BREWERY | TYPE / STYLE |
|---|---|
| ABV | IBU |
| ORIGIN | SAMPLED |

## SERVING TYPE

| CAN | BOTTLE | CASK | DRAFT | GROWLER | MIXED | OTHER |
|---|---|---|---|---|---|---|
| ☐ | ☐ | ☐ | ☐ | ☐ | ☐ | ☐ |

## BUBBLES & COLOR

HIGH

SPARKLING

MEDIUM

STILL

PALE AMBER

MEDIUM AMBER

DEEP AMBER

AMBER BROWN

BROWN

ERUBY BROWN

## FLAVOR WHEEL

CREAMY · SWEET · EARTHY · HERBAL · FLORAL · SPICY · BITTER · SOUR · HOPPY · MALTY · TOASTED · FRUITY · CARAMEL · COFFEE · NUTTY · DAIRY

## FINAL RATING

APPEARANCE ☆☆☆☆☆

AROMA ☆☆☆☆☆

TASTE ☆☆☆☆☆

MOUTHFEEL ☆☆☆☆☆

OVERALL RATING ☆☆☆☆☆

## ADDITIONAL NOTES

## NAME

| BREWERY | TYPE / STYLE |
|---|---|
| ABV | IBU |
| ORIGIN | SAMPLED |

## SERVING TYPE

| CAN | BOTTLE | CASK | DRAFT | GROWLER | MIXED | OTHER |
|---|---|---|---|---|---|---|
| ☐ | ☐ | ☐ | ☐ | ☐ | ☐ | ☐ |

## BUBBLES & COLOR

HIGH

SPARKLING

MEDIUM

STILL

PALE AMBER

MEDIUM AMBER

DEEP AMBER

AMBER BROWN

BROWN

ERUBY BROWN

## FLAVOR WHEEL

CREAMY — SWEET — EARTHY — HERBAL — FLORAL — SPICY — BITTER — SOUR — HOPPY — MALTY — TOASTED — FRUITY — CARAMEL — COFFEE — NUTTY — DAIRY

## FINAL RATING

| APPEARANCE | ☆☆☆☆☆ |
|---|---|
| AROMA | ☆☆☆☆☆ |
| TASTE | ☆☆☆☆☆ |
| MOUTHFEEL | ☆☆☆☆☆ |
| OVERALL RATING | ☆☆☆☆☆ |

## ADDITIONAL NOTES

## NAME

## BREWERY

## TYPE / STYLE

## ABV

## IBU

## ORIGIN

## SAMPLED

## SERVING TYPE

| CAN | BOTTLE | CASK | DRAFT | GROWLER | MIXED | OTHER |
|-----|--------|------|-------|---------|-------|-------|
| ☐ | ☐ | ☐ | ☐ | ☐ | ☐ | ☐ |

## BUBBLES & COLOR

HIGH

SPARKLING

MEDIUM

STILL

PALE AMBER

MEDIUM AMBER

DEEP AMBER

AMBER BROWN

BROWN

ERUBY BROWN

## FLAVOR WHEEL

CREAMY
SWEET
EARTHY
HERBAL
DAIRY
FLORAL
NUTTY
SPICY
COFFEE
BITTER
CARAMEL
SOUR
FRUITY
HOPPY
TOASTED
MALTY

## FINAL RATING

| APPEARANCE | ☆☆☆☆☆ |
|------------|-------|
| AROMA | ☆☆☆☆☆ |
| TASTE | ☆☆☆☆☆ |
| MOUTHFEEL | ☆☆☆☆☆ |
| OVERALL RATING | ☆☆☆☆☆ |

## ADDITIONAL NOTES

## NAME

| | | | |
|---|---|---|---|
| **BREWERY** | | **TYPE / STYLE** | |
| **ABV** | | **IBU** | |
| **ORIGIN** | | **SAMPLED** | |

## SERVING TYPE

| CAN | BOTTLE | CASK | DRAFT | GROWLER | MIXED | OTHER |
|---|---|---|---|---|---|---|
| ☐ | ☐ | ☐ | ☐ | ☐ | ☐ | ☐ |

## BUBBLES & COLOR

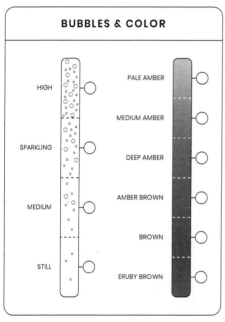

HIGH

SPARKLING

MEDIUM

STILL

PALE AMBER

MEDIUM AMBER

DEEP AMBER

AMBER BROWN

BROWN

ERUBY BROWN

## FLAVOR WHEEL

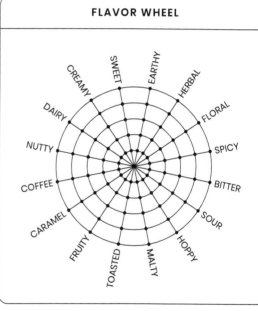

CREAMY · SWEET · EARTHY · HERBAL · FLORAL · SPICY · BITTER · SOUR · HOPPY · MALTY · TOASTED · FRUITY · CARAMEL · COFFEE · NUTTY · DAIRY

## FINAL RATING

| | | |
|---|---|---|
| APPEARANCE | ☆☆☆☆☆ |
| AROMA | ☆☆☆☆☆ |
| TASTE | ☆☆☆☆☆ |
| MOUTHFEEL | ☆☆☆☆☆ |
| OVERALL RATING | ☆☆☆☆☆ |

## ADDITIONAL NOTES

## NAME

| BREWERY | TYPE / STYLE |
|---|---|
| ABV | IBU |
| ORIGIN | SAMPLED |

## SERVING TYPE

| CAN | BOTTLE | CASK | DRAFT | GROWLER | MIXED | OTHER |
|---|---|---|---|---|---|---|
| ☐ | ☐ | ☐ | ☐ | ☐ | ☐ | ☐ |

## BUBBLES & COLOR

HIGH

SPARKLING

MEDIUM

STILL

PALE AMBER ○
MEDIUM AMBER ○
DEEP AMBER ○
AMBER BROWN ○
BROWN ○
ERUBY BROWN ○

## FLAVOR WHEEL

CREAMY · SWEET · EARTHY · HERBAL · FLORAL · SPICY · BITTER · SOUR · HOPPY · MALTY · TOASTED · FRUITY · CARAMEL · COFFEE · NUTTY · DAIRY

## FINAL RATING

| APPEARANCE | ☆☆☆☆☆ |
|---|---|
| AROMA | ☆☆☆☆☆ |
| TASTE | ☆☆☆☆☆ |
| MOUTHFEEL | ☆☆☆☆☆ |
| OVERALL RATING | ☆☆☆☆☆ |

## ADDITIONAL NOTES

## NAME

| BREWERY | TYPE / STYLE |
|---|---|
| ABV | IBU |
| ORIGIN | SAMPLED |

## SERVING TYPE

| CAN | BOTTLE | CASK | DRAFT | GROWLER | MIXED | OTHER |
|---|---|---|---|---|---|---|
| ☐ | ☐ | ☐ | ☐ | ☐ | ☐ | ☐ |

## BUBBLES & COLOR

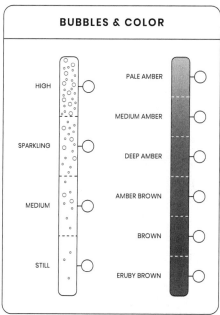

HIGH

SPARKLING

MEDIUM

STILL

PALE AMBER

MEDIUM AMBER

DEEP AMBER

AMBER BROWN

BROWN

ERUBY BROWN

## FLAVOR WHEEL

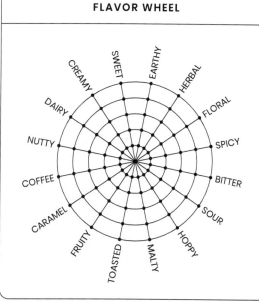

CREAMY · SWEET · EARTHY · HERBAL · FLORAL · SPICY · BITTER · SOUR · HOPPY · MALTY · TOASTED · FRUITY · CARAMEL · COFFEE · NUTTY · DAIRY

## FINAL RATING

| APPEARANCE | ☆☆☆☆☆ |
|---|---|
| AROMA | ☆☆☆☆☆ |
| TASTE | ☆☆☆☆☆ |
| MOUTHFEEL | ☆☆☆☆☆ |
| OVERALL RATING | ☆☆☆☆☆ |

## ADDITIONAL NOTES

## NAME

## BREWERY

## TYPE / STYLE

## ABV

## IBU

## ORIGIN

## SAMPLED

## SERVING TYPE

| CAN | BOTTLE | CASK | DRAFT | GROWLER | MIXED | OTHER |
|-----|--------|------|-------|---------|-------|-------|
| ☐ | ☐ | ☐ | ☐ | ☐ | ☐ | ☐ |

## BUBBLES & COLOR

HIGH

SPARKLING

MEDIUM

STILL

PALE AMBER

MEDIUM AMBER

DEEP AMBER

AMBER BROWN

BROWN

ERUBY BROWN

## FLAVOR WHEEL

CREAMY · SWEET · EARTHY · HERBAL · FLORAL · SPICY · BITTER · SOUR · HOPPY · MALTY · TOASTED · FRUITY · CARAMEL · COFFEE · NUTTY · DAIRY

## FINAL RATING

APPEARANCE ☆☆☆☆☆

AROMA ☆☆☆☆☆

TASTE ☆☆☆☆☆

MOUTHFEEL ☆☆☆☆☆

OVERALL RATING ☆☆☆☆☆

## ADDITIONAL NOTES

## NAME

| BREWERY | TYPE / STYLE |
|---|---|
| ABV | IBU |
| ORIGIN | SAMPLED |

## SERVING TYPE

| CAN | BOTTLE | CASK | DRAFT | GROWLER | MIXED | OTHER |
|---|---|---|---|---|---|---|
| ☐ | ☐ | ☐ | ☐ | ☐ | ☐ | ☐ |

## BUBBLES & COLOR

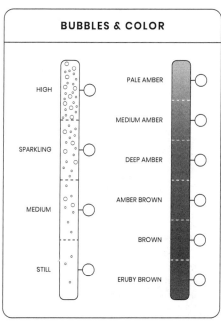

HIGH

SPARKLING

MEDIUM

STILL

PALE AMBER
MEDIUM AMBER
DEEP AMBER
AMBER BROWN
BROWN
ERUBY BROWN

## FLAVOR WHEEL

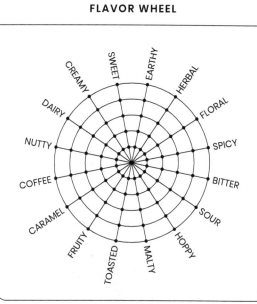

CREAMY · SWEET · EARTHY · HERBAL · FLORAL · SPICY · BITTER · SOUR · HOPPY · MALTY · TOASTED · FRUITY · CARAMEL · COFFEE · NUTTY · DAIRY

## FINAL RATING

| APPEARANCE | ☆☆☆☆☆ |
|---|---|
| AROMA | ☆☆☆☆☆ |
| TASTE | ☆☆☆☆☆ |
| MOUTHFEEL | ☆☆☆☆☆ |
| OVERALL RATING | ☆☆☆☆☆ |

## ADDITIONAL NOTES

| 🍺 NAME | |
|---|---|
| 🛢 BREWERY | 🍶 TYPE / STYLE |
| 🍾 ABV | 🌿 IBU |
| 🌍 ORIGIN | 📅 SAMPLED |

## SERVING TYPE

| CAN | BOTTLE | CASK | DRAFT | GROWLER | MIXED | OTHER |
|---|---|---|---|---|---|---|
| 📱 ☐ | 🍾 ☐ | 🛢 ☐ | 🍺 ☐ | 🥤 ☐ | 🍹 ☐ | ⚗ ☐ |

## BUBBLES & COLOR

HIGH

SPARKLING

MEDIUM

STILL

PALE AMBER
MEDIUM AMBER
DEEP AMBER
AMBER BROWN
BROWN
ERUBY BROWN

## FLAVOR WHEEL

CREAMY · SWEET · EARTHY · HERBAL · FLORAL · SPICY · BITTER · SOUR · HOPPY · MALTY · TOASTED · FRUITY · CARAMEL · COFFEE · NUTTY · DAIRY

## FINAL RATING

| 🍾 APPEARANCE | ☆☆☆☆☆ |
|---|---|
| 🌾 AROMA | ☆☆☆☆☆ |
| 🍺 TASTE | ☆☆☆☆☆ |
| 👄 MOUTHFEEL | ☆☆☆☆☆ |
| 🏆 OVERALL RATING | ☆☆☆☆☆ |

## ADDITIONAL NOTES

## NAME

| BREWERY | TYPE / STYLE |
|---|---|
| ABV | IBU |
| ORIGIN | SAMPLED |

## SERVING TYPE

| CAN | BOTTLE | CASK | DRAFT | GROWLER | MIXED | OTHER |
|---|---|---|---|---|---|---|
| ☐ | ☐ | ☐ | ☐ | ☐ | ☐ | ☐ |

## BUBBLES & COLOR

HIGH

SPARKLING

MEDIUM

STILL

PALE AMBER
MEDIUM AMBER
DEEP AMBER
AMBER BROWN
BROWN
ERUBY BROWN

## FLAVOR WHEEL

CREAMY · SWEET · EARTHY · HERBAL · FLORAL · SPICY · BITTER · SOUR · HOPPY · MALTY · TOASTED · FRUITY · CARAMEL · COFFEE · NUTTY · DAIRY

## FINAL RATING

| APPEARANCE | ☆☆☆☆☆ |
|---|---|
| AROMA | ☆☆☆☆☆ |
| TASTE | ☆☆☆☆☆ |
| MOUTHFEEL | ☆☆☆☆☆ |
| OVERALL RATING | ☆☆☆☆☆ |

## ADDITIONAL NOTES

| 🍺 NAME | |
|---|---|
| 🛢 BREWERY | 🍾 TYPE / STYLE |
| 🥃 ABV | 🌿 IBU |
| 🌍 ORIGIN | 📅 SAMPLED |

## SERVING TYPE

| CAN | BOTTLE | CASK | DRAFT | GROWLER | MIXED | OTHER |
|---|---|---|---|---|---|---|
| ☐ | ☐ | ☐ | ☐ | ☐ | ☐ | ☐ |

## BUBBLES & COLOR

HIGH

SPARKLING

MEDIUM

STILL

PALE AMBER

MEDIUM AMBER

DEEP AMBER

AMBER BROWN

BROWN

ERUBY BROWN

## FLAVOR WHEEL

CREAMY · SWEET · EARTHY · HERBAL · FLORAL · SPICY · BITTER · SOUR · HOPPY · MALTY · TOASTED · FRUITY · CARAMEL · COFFEE · NUTTY · DAIRY

## FINAL RATING

| 🍾 APPEARANCE | ☆☆☆☆☆ |
|---|---|
| 🌾 AROMA | ☆☆☆☆☆ |
| 🍺 TASTE | ☆☆☆☆☆ |
| 👄 MOUTHFEEL | ☆☆☆☆☆ |
| 🙌 OVERALL RATING | ☆☆☆☆☆ |

## ADDITIONAL NOTES

## NAME

| BREWERY | TYPE / STYLE |
|---|---|
| ABV | IBU |
| ORIGIN | SAMPLED |

## SERVING TYPE

| CAN | BOTTLE | CASK | DRAFT | GROWLER | MIXED | OTHER |
|---|---|---|---|---|---|---|
| ☐ | ☐ | ☐ | ☐ | ☐ | ☐ | ☐ |

## BUBBLES & COLOR

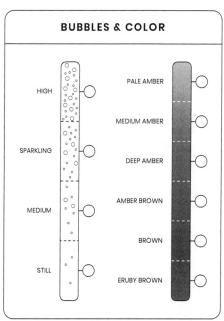

HIGH

SPARKLING

MEDIUM

STILL

PALE AMBER

MEDIUM AMBER

DEEP AMBER

AMBER BROWN

BROWN

ERUBY BROWN

## FLAVOR WHEEL

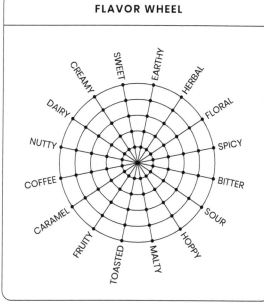

CREAMY · SWEET · EARTHY · HERBAL · DAIRY · FLORAL · NUTTY · SPICY · COFFEE · BITTER · CARAMEL · SOUR · FRUITY · HOPPY · TOASTED · MALTY

## FINAL RATING

| APPEARANCE | ☆☆☆☆☆ |
|---|---|
| AROMA | ☆☆☆☆☆ |
| TASTE | ☆☆☆☆☆ |
| MOUTHFEEL | ☆☆☆☆☆ |
| OVERALL RATING | ☆☆☆☆☆ |

## ADDITIONAL NOTES

## NAME

## BREWERY

## ABV

## ORIGIN

## TYPE / STYLE

## IBU

## SAMPLED

## SERVING TYPE

| CAN | BOTTLE | CASK | DRAFT | GROWLER | MIXED | OTHER |
|-----|--------|------|-------|---------|-------|-------|
| ☐ | ☐ | ☐ | ☐ | ☐ | ☐ | ☐ |

## BUBBLES & COLOR

HIGH

SPARKLING

MEDIUM

STILL

PALE AMBER
MEDIUM AMBER
DEEP AMBER
AMBER BROWN
BROWN
ERUBY BROWN

## FLAVOR WHEEL

CREAMY · SWEET · EARTHY · HERBAL · FLORAL · SPICY · BITTER · SOUR · HOPPY · MALTY · TOASTED · FRUITY · CARAMEL · COFFEE · NUTTY · DAIRY

## FINAL RATING

| APPEARANCE | ☆☆☆☆☆ |
|------------|--------|
| AROMA | ☆☆☆☆☆ |
| TASTE | ☆☆☆☆☆ |
| MOUTHFEEL | ☆☆☆☆☆ |
| OVERALL RATING | ☆☆☆☆☆ |

## ADDITIONAL NOTES

## NAME

| BREWERY | TYPE / STYLE |
|---|---|
| ABV | IBU |
| ORIGIN | SAMPLED |

## SERVING TYPE

| CAN | BOTTLE | CASK | DRAFT | GROWLER | MIXED | OTHER |
|---|---|---|---|---|---|---|
| ☐ | ☐ | ☐ | ☐ | ☐ | ☐ | ☐ |

## BUBBLES & COLOR

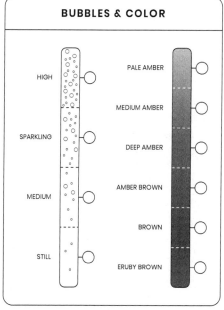

HIGH

SPARKLING

MEDIUM

STILL

PALE AMBER

MEDIUM AMBER

DEEP AMBER

AMBER BROWN

BROWN

ERUBY BROWN

## FLAVOR WHEEL

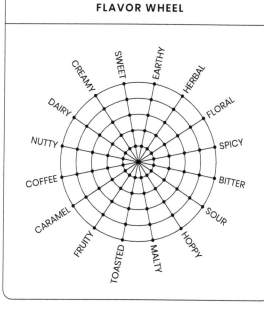

CREAMY · SWEET · EARTHY · HERBAL · FLORAL · SPICY · BITTER · SOUR · HOPPY · MALTY · TOASTED · FRUITY · CARAMEL · COFFEE · NUTTY · DAIRY

## FINAL RATING

| APPEARANCE | ☆☆☆☆☆ |
|---|---|
| AROMA | ☆☆☆☆☆ |
| TASTE | ☆☆☆☆☆ |
| MOUTHFEEL | ☆☆☆☆☆ |
| OVERALL RATING | ☆☆☆☆☆ |

## ADDITIONAL NOTES

## NAME

## BREWERY

## TYPE / STYLE

## ABV

## IBU

## ORIGIN

## SAMPLED

## SERVING TYPE

| CAN | BOTTLE | CASK | DRAFT | GROWLER | MIXED | OTHER |
|-----|--------|------|-------|---------|-------|-------|
| ☐ | ☐ | ☐ | ☐ | ☐ | ☐ | ☐ |

## BUBBLES & COLOR

HIGH

SPARKLING

MEDIUM

STILL

PALE AMBER

MEDIUM AMBER

DEEP AMBER

AMBER BROWN

BROWN

ERUBY BROWN

## FLAVOR WHEEL

CREAMY · SWEET · EARTHY · HERBAL · FLORAL · SPICY · BITTER · SOUR · HOPPY · MALTY · TOASTED · FRUITY · CARAMEL · COFFEE · NUTTY · DAIRY

## FINAL RATING

| APPEARANCE | ☆☆☆☆☆ |
|------------|-------|
| AROMA | ☆☆☆☆☆ |
| TASTE | ☆☆☆☆☆ |
| MOUTHFEEL | ☆☆☆☆☆ |
| OVERALL RATING | ☆☆☆☆☆ |

## ADDITIONAL NOTES

## NAME

| BREWERY | TYPE / STYLE |
|---|---|
| ABV | IBU |
| ORIGIN | SAMPLED |

## SERVING TYPE

| CAN | BOTTLE | CASK | DRAFT | GROWLER | MIXED | OTHER |
|---|---|---|---|---|---|---|
| ☐ | ☐ | ☐ | ☐ | ☐ | ☐ | ☐ |

## BUBBLES & COLOR

HIGH

SPARKLING

MEDIUM

STILL

PALE AMBER

MEDIUM AMBER

DEEP AMBER

AMBER BROWN

BROWN

ERUBY BROWN

## FLAVOR WHEEL

CREAMY · SWEET · EARTHY · HERBAL · FLORAL · SPICY · BITTER · SOUR · HOPPY · MALTY · TOASTED · FRUITY · CARAMEL · COFFEE · NUTTY · DAIRY

## FINAL RATING

| APPEARANCE | ☆☆☆☆☆ |
|---|---|
| AROMA | ☆☆☆☆☆ |
| TASTE | ☆☆☆☆☆ |
| MOUTHFEEL | ☆☆☆☆☆ |
| OVERALL RATING | ☆☆☆☆☆ |

## ADDITIONAL NOTES

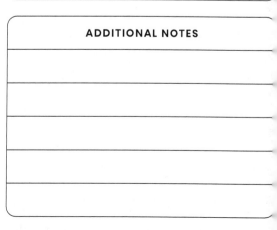

## NAME

| | |
|---|---|
| **BREWERY** | **TYPE / STYLE** |
| **ABV** | **IBU** |
| **ORIGIN** | **SAMPLED** |

## SERVING TYPE

| CAN | BOTTLE | CASK | DRAFT | GROWLER | MIXED | OTHER |
|---|---|---|---|---|---|---|
| ☐ | ☐ | ☐ | ☐ | ☐ | ☐ | ☐ |

## BUBBLES & COLOR

HIGH

SPARKLING

MEDIUM

STILL

PALE AMBER

MEDIUM AMBER

DEEP AMBER

AMBER BROWN

BROWN

ERUBY BROWN

## FLAVOR WHEEL

CREAMY · SWEET · EARTHY · HERBAL · FLORAL · SPICY · BITTER · SOUR · HOPPY · MALTY · TOASTED · FRUITY · CARAMEL · COFFEE · NUTTY · DAIRY

## FINAL RATING

| | | |
|---|---|---|
| APPEARANCE | ☆☆☆☆☆ |
| AROMA | ☆☆☆☆☆ |
| TASTE | ☆☆☆☆☆ |
| MOUTHFEEL | ☆☆☆☆☆ |
| OVERALL RATING | ☆☆☆☆☆ |

## ADDITIONAL NOTES

## NAME

| BREWERY | TYPE / STYLE |
|---|---|
| ABV | IBU |
| ORIGIN | SAMPLED |

## SERVING TYPE

| CAN | BOTTLE | CASK | DRAFT | GROWLER | MIXED | OTHER |
|---|---|---|---|---|---|---|
| ☐ | ☐ | ☐ | ☐ | ☐ | ☐ | ☐ |

## BUBBLES & COLOR

HIGH

SPARKLING

MEDIUM

STILL

PALE AMBER

MEDIUM AMBER

DEEP AMBER

AMBER BROWN

BROWN

ERUBY BROWN

## FLAVOR WHEEL

CREAMY · SWEET · EARTHY · HERBAL · DAIRY · FLORAL · NUTTY · SPICY · COFFEE · BITTER · CARAMEL · SOUR · FRUITY · HOPPY · TOASTED · MALTY

## FINAL RATING

| APPEARANCE | ☆☆☆☆☆ |
|---|---|
| AROMA | ☆☆☆☆☆ |
| TASTE | ☆☆☆☆☆ |
| MOUTHFEEL | ☆☆☆☆☆ |
| OVERALL RATING | ☆☆☆☆☆ |

## ADDITIONAL NOTES

## NAME

| BREWERY | TYPE / STYLE |
|---|---|
| ABV | IBU |
| ORIGIN | SAMPLED |

## SERVING TYPE

| CAN | BOTTLE | CASK | DRAFT | GROWLER | MIXED | OTHER |
|---|---|---|---|---|---|---|
| ☐ | ☐ | ☐ | ☐ | ☐ | ☐ | ☐ |

## BUBBLES & COLOR

HIGH

SPARKLING

MEDIUM

STILL

PALE AMBER

MEDIUM AMBER

DEEP AMBER

AMBER BROWN

BROWN

ERUBY BROWN

## FLAVOR WHEEL

CREAMY · SWEET · EARTHY · HERBAL · FLORAL · SPICY · BITTER · SOUR · HOPPY · MALTY · TOASTED · FRUITY · CARAMEL · COFFEE · NUTTY · DAIRY

## FINAL RATING

| APPEARANCE | ☆☆☆☆☆ |
|---|---|
| AROMA | ☆☆☆☆☆ |
| TASTE | ☆☆☆☆☆ |
| MOUTHFEEL | ☆☆☆☆☆ |
| OVERALL RATING | ☆☆☆☆☆ |

## ADDITIONAL NOTES

## NAME

| BREWERY | TYPE / STYLE |
|---|---|
| ABV | IBU |
| ORIGIN | SAMPLED |

## SERVING TYPE

| CAN | BOTTLE | CASK | DRAFT | GROWLER | MIXED | OTHER |
|---|---|---|---|---|---|---|
| ☐ | ☐ | ☐ | ☐ | ☐ | ☐ | ☐ |

## BUBBLES & COLOR

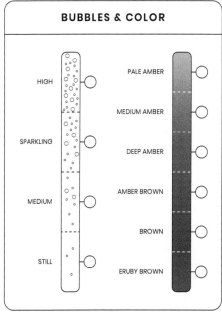

HIGH

SPARKLING

MEDIUM

STILL

PALE AMBER

MEDIUM AMBER

DEEP AMBER

AMBER BROWN

BROWN

ERUBY BROWN

## FLAVOR WHEEL

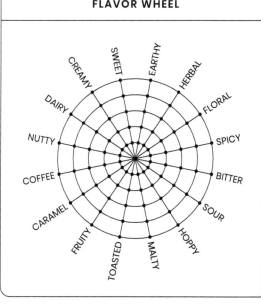

CREAMY — SWEET — EARTHY — HERBAL — FLORAL — SPICY — BITTER — SOUR — HOPPY — MALTY — TOASTED — FRUITY — CARAMEL — COFFEE — NUTTY — DAIRY

## FINAL RATING

| APPEARANCE | ☆☆☆☆☆ |
|---|---|
| AROMA | ☆☆☆☆☆ |
| TASTE | ☆☆☆☆☆ |
| MOUTHFEEL | ☆☆☆☆☆ |
| OVERALL RATING | ☆☆☆☆☆ |

## ADDITIONAL NOTES

# NAME

| BREWERY | TYPE / STYLE |
|---|---|
| ABV | IBU |
| ORIGIN | SAMPLED |

## SERVING TYPE

| CAN | BOTTLE | CASK | DRAFT | GROWLER | MIXED | OTHER |
|---|---|---|---|---|---|---|
| ☐ | ☐ | ☐ | ☐ | ☐ | ☐ | ☐ |

## BUBBLES & COLOR

HIGH

SPARKLING

MEDIUM

STILL

PALE AMBER

MEDIUM AMBER

DEEP AMBER

AMBER BROWN

BROWN

ERUBY BROWN

## FLAVOR WHEEL

CREAMY · SWEET · EARTHY · HERBAL · FLORAL · SPICY · BITTER · SOUR · HOPPY · MALTY · TOASTED · FRUITY · CARAMEL · COFFEE · NUTTY · DAIRY

## FINAL RATING

| APPEARANCE | ☆☆☆☆☆ |
|---|---|
| AROMA | ☆☆☆☆☆ |
| TASTE | ☆☆☆☆☆ |
| MOUTHFEEL | ☆☆☆☆☆ |
| OVERALL RATING | ☆☆☆☆☆ |

## ADDITIONAL NOTES

| 🍺 **NAME** | |
|---|---|
| 🛢️ **BREWERY** | 🍾 **TYPE / STYLE** |
| 🍶 **ABV** | 🌺 **IBU** |
| 🌍 **ORIGIN** | 📅 **SAMPLED** |

## SERVING TYPE

| CAN | BOTTLE | CASK | DRAFT | GROWLER | MIXED | OTHER |
|---|---|---|---|---|---|---|
| 🥫 | 🍾 | 🛢️ | 🍺 | 🧃 | 🍹 | ⚗️ |
| ☐ | ☐ | ☐ | ☐ | ☐ | ☐ | ☐ |

## BUBBLES & COLOR

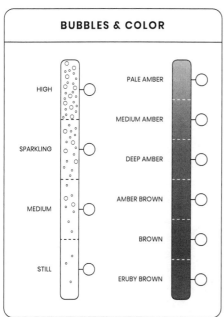

HIGH

SPARKLING

MEDIUM

STILL

PALE AMBER

MEDIUM AMBER

DEEP AMBER

AMBER BROWN

BROWN

ERUBY BROWN

## FLAVOR WHEEL

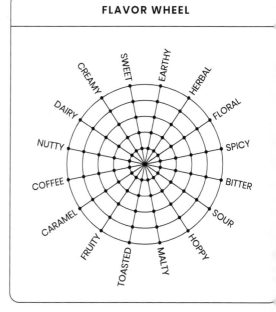

CREAMY · SWEET · EARTHY · HERBAL · DAIRY · FLORAL · NUTTY · SPICY · COFFEE · BITTER · CARAMEL · SOUR · FRUITY · HOPPY · TOASTED · MALTY

## FINAL RATING

| | | |
|---|---|---|
| 🍾 | APPEARANCE | ☆☆☆☆☆ |
| 🌾 | AROMA | ☆☆☆☆☆ |
| 🍺 | TASTE | ☆☆☆☆☆ |
| 👄 | MOUTHFEEL | ☆☆☆☆☆ |
| ☆ | OVERALL RATING | ☆☆☆☆☆ |

## ADDITIONAL NOTES

# NAME

| | |
|---|---|
| BREWERY | TYPE / STYLE |
| ABV | IBU |
| ORIGIN | SAMPLED |

## SERVING TYPE

| CAN | BOTTLE | CASK | DRAFT | GROWLER | MIXED | OTHER |
|---|---|---|---|---|---|---|
| ☐ | ☐ | ☐ | ☐ | ☐ | ☐ | ☐ |

## BUBBLES & COLOR

HIGH

SPARKLING

MEDIUM

STILL

PALE AMBER

MEDIUM AMBER

DEEP AMBER

AMBER BROWN

BROWN

ERUBY BROWN

## FLAVOR WHEEL

CREAMY SWEET EARTHY HERBAL FLORAL SPICY BITTER SOUR HOPPY MALTY TOASTED FRUITY CARAMEL COFFEE NUTTY DAIRY

## FINAL RATING

| | |
|---|---|
| APPEARANCE | ☆☆☆☆☆ |
| AROMA | ☆☆☆☆☆ |
| TASTE | ☆☆☆☆☆ |
| MOUTHFEEL | ☆☆☆☆☆ |
| OVERALL RATING | ☆☆☆☆☆ |

## ADDITIONAL NOTES

## NAME

| 🍺 BREWERY | 🧴 TYPE / STYLE |
|---|---|
| 🥃 ABV | 🌿 IBU |
| 🌍 ORIGIN | 📅 SAMPLED |

## SERVING TYPE

| CAN | BOTTLE | CASK | DRAFT | GROWLER | MIXED | OTHER |
|---|---|---|---|---|---|---|
| ☐ | ☐ | ☐ | ☐ | ☐ | ☐ | ☐ |

## BUBBLES & COLOR

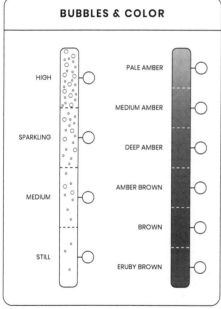

HIGH
SPARKLING
MEDIUM
STILL

PALE AMBER
MEDIUM AMBER
DEEP AMBER
AMBER BROWN
BROWN
ERUBY BROWN

## FLAVOR WHEEL

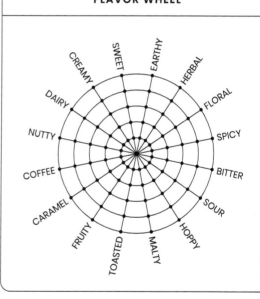

CREAMY · SWEET · EARTHY · HERBAL · DAIRY · FLORAL · NUTTY · SPICY · COFFEE · BITTER · CARAMEL · SOUR · FRUITY · HOPPY · TOASTED · MALTY

## FINAL RATING

| | | |
|---|---|---|
| 🍾 APPEARANCE | ☆☆☆☆☆ |
| 🌾 AROMA | ☆☆☆☆☆ |
| 🍺 TASTE | ☆☆☆☆☆ |
| 👄 MOUTHFEEL | ☆☆☆☆☆ |
| ✋ OVERALL RATING | ☆☆☆☆☆ |

## ADDITIONAL NOTES

## NAME

| BREWERY | TYPE / STYLE |
|---|---|
| ABV | IBU |
| ORIGIN | SAMPLED |

## SERVING TYPE

| CAN | BOTTLE | CASK | DRAFT | GROWLER | MIXED | OTHER |
|---|---|---|---|---|---|---|
| ☐ | ☐ | ☐ | ☐ | ☐ | ☐ | ☐ |

## BUBBLES & COLOR

HIGH

SPARKLING

MEDIUM

STILL

PALE AMBER ○

MEDIUM AMBER ○

DEEP AMBER ○

AMBER BROWN ○

BROWN ○

ERUBY BROWN ○

## FLAVOR WHEEL

CREAMY · SWEET · EARTHY · HERBAL · FLORAL · SPICY · BITTER · SOUR · HOPPY · MALTY · TOASTED · FRUITY · CARAMEL · COFFEE · NUTTY · DAIRY

## FINAL RATING

| APPEARANCE | ☆☆☆☆☆ |
|---|---|
| AROMA | ☆☆☆☆☆ |
| TASTE | ☆☆☆☆☆ |
| MOUTHFEEL | ☆☆☆☆☆ |
| OVERALL RATING | ☆☆☆☆☆ |

## ADDITIONAL NOTES

| 🍺 NAME | |
|---|---|
| 🛢 BREWERY | 🍾 TYPE / STYLE |
| 🍾 ABV | 🌺 IBU |
| 🌍 ORIGIN | 📅 SAMPLED |

## SERVING TYPE

| CAN | BOTTLE | CASK | DRAFT | GROWLER | MIXED | OTHER |
|---|---|---|---|---|---|---|
| 🥫 ☐ | 🍾 ☐ | 🛢 ☐ | 🍺 ☐ | 🫗 ☐ | 🍹 ☐ | ⚗ ☐ |

## BUBBLES & COLOR

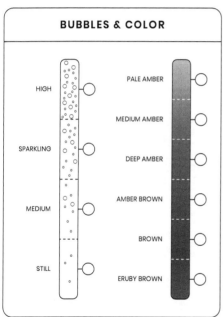

HIGH

SPARKLING

MEDIUM

STILL

PALE AMBER

MEDIUM AMBER

DEEP AMBER

AMBER BROWN

BROWN

ERUBY BROWN

## FLAVOR WHEEL

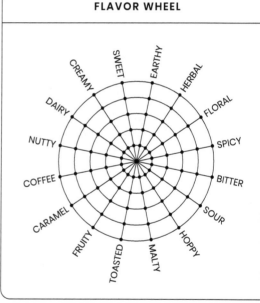

CREAMY · SWEET · EARTHY · HERBAL · DAIRY · FLORAL · NUTTY · SPICY · COFFEE · BITTER · CARAMEL · SOUR · FRUITY · HOPPY · TOASTED · MALTY

## FINAL RATING

| | | |
|---|---|---|
| 🍾 APPEARANCE | ☆☆☆☆☆ |
| 🌾 AROMA | ☆☆☆☆☆ |
| 🍺 TASTE | ☆☆☆☆☆ |
| 👄 MOUTHFEEL | ☆☆☆☆☆ |
| ✋ OVERALL RATING | ☆☆☆☆☆ |

## ADDITIONAL NOTES

## NAME

| BREWERY | TYPE / STYLE |
|---|---|
| ABV | IBU |
| ORIGIN | SAMPLED |

## SERVING TYPE

| CAN | BOTTLE | CASK | DRAFT | GROWLER | MIXED | OTHER |
|---|---|---|---|---|---|---|
| ☐ | ☐ | ☐ | ☐ | ☐ | ☐ | ☐ |

## BUBBLES & COLOR

HIGH

SPARKLING

MEDIUM

STILL

PALE AMBER ◯
MEDIUM AMBER ◯
DEEP AMBER ◯
AMBER BROWN ◯
BROWN ◯
ERUBY BROWN ◯

## FLAVOR WHEEL

CREAMY SWEET EARTHY HERBAL
DAIRY FLORAL
NUTTY SPICY
COFFEE BITTER
CARAMEL SOUR
FRUITY TOASTED MALTY HOPPY

## FINAL RATING

| APPEARANCE | ☆☆☆☆☆ |
|---|---|
| AROMA | ☆☆☆☆☆ |
| TASTE | ☆☆☆☆☆ |
| MOUTHFEEL | ☆☆☆☆☆ |
| OVERALL RATING | ☆☆☆☆☆ |

## ADDITIONAL NOTES

## NAME

| | | | |
|---|---|---|---|
| BREWERY | | TYPE / STYLE | |
| ABV | | IBU | |
| ORIGIN | | SAMPLED | |

## SERVING TYPE

| CAN | BOTTLE | CASK | DRAFT | GROWLER | MIXED | OTHER |
|---|---|---|---|---|---|---|
| ☐ | ☐ | ☐ | ☐ | ☐ | ☐ | ☐ |

## BUBBLES & COLOR

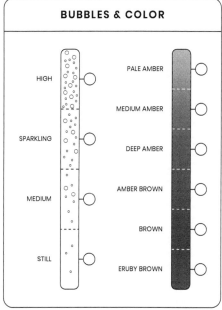

HIGH
SPARKLING
MEDIUM
STILL

PALE AMBER
MEDIUM AMBER
DEEP AMBER
AMBER BROWN
BROWN
ERUBY BROWN

## FLAVOR WHEEL

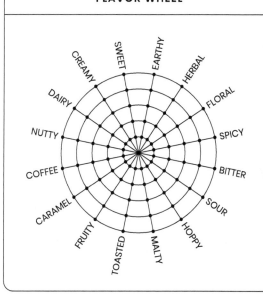

CREAMY · SWEET · EARTHY · HERBAL · DAIRY · FLORAL · NUTTY · SPICY · COFFEE · BITTER · CARAMEL · SOUR · FRUITY · HOPPY · TOASTED · MALTY

## FINAL RATING

| | | |
|---|---|---|
| APPEARANCE | ☆☆☆☆☆ |
| AROMA | ☆☆☆☆☆ |
| TASTE | ☆☆☆☆☆ |
| MOUTHFEEL | ☆☆☆☆☆ |
| OVERALL RATING | ☆☆☆☆☆ |

## ADDITIONAL NOTES

# NAME

| | |
|---|---|
| **BREWERY** | **TYPE / STYLE** |
| **ABV** | **IBU** |
| **ORIGIN** | **SAMPLED** |

## SERVING TYPE

| CAN | BOTTLE | CASK | DRAFT | GROWLER | MIXED | OTHER |
|---|---|---|---|---|---|---|
| ☐ | ☐ | ☐ | ☐ | ☐ | ☐ | ☐ |

## BUBBLES & COLOR

HIGH

SPARKLING

MEDIUM

STILL

PALE AMBER

MEDIUM AMBER

DEEP AMBER

AMBER BROWN

BROWN

ERUBY BROWN

## FLAVOR WHEEL

CREAMY
SWEET
EARTHY
HERBAL
DAIRY
FLORAL
NUTTY
SPICY
COFFEE
BITTER
CARAMEL
SOUR
FRUITY
HOPPY
TOASTED
MALTY

## FINAL RATING

| | | |
|---|---|---|
| APPEARANCE | ☆☆☆☆☆ |
| AROMA | ☆☆☆☆☆ |
| TASTE | ☆☆☆☆☆ |
| MOUTHFEEL | ☆☆☆☆☆ |
| OVERALL RATING | ☆☆☆☆☆ |

## ADDITIONAL NOTES

| 🍺 NAME | |
|---|---|
| 🛢 BREWERY | 🍾 TYPE / STYLE |
| 🍶 ABV | 🌿 IBU |
| 🌍 ORIGIN | 📅 SAMPLED |

## SERVING TYPE

| CAN | BOTTLE | CASK | DRAFT | GROWLER | MIXED | OTHER |
|---|---|---|---|---|---|---|
| 🥫 ☐ | 🍾 ☐ | 🛢 ☐ | 🍺 ☐ | 🫗 ☐ | 🍹 ☐ | ⚗ ☐ |

## BUBBLES & COLOR

HIGH

SPARKLING

MEDIUM

STILL

PALE AMBER

MEDIUM AMBER

DEEP AMBER

AMBER BROWN

BROWN

ERUBY BROWN

## FLAVOR WHEEL

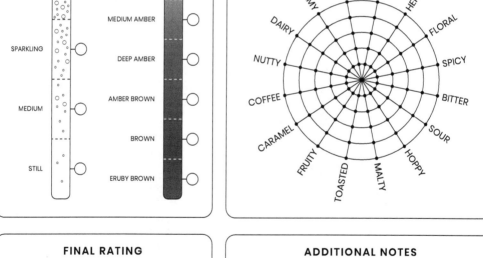

CREAMY · SWEET · EARTHY · HERBAL · FLORAL · SPICY · BITTER · SOUR · HOPPY · MALTY · TOASTED · FRUITY · CARAMEL · COFFEE · NUTTY · DAIRY

## FINAL RATING

| 🍾 APPEARANCE | ☆☆☆☆☆ |
|---|---|
| 🌾 AROMA | ☆☆☆☆☆ |
| 🍺 TASTE | ☆☆☆☆☆ |
| 👄 MOUTHFEEL | ☆☆☆☆☆ |
| 🙌 OVERALL RATING | ☆☆☆☆☆ |

## ADDITIONAL NOTES

| 🍺 NAME | |
|---|---|
| 🛢 **BREWERY** | 🍾 **TYPE / STYLE** |
| 🥃 **ABV** | 🌿 **IBU** |
| 🌍 **ORIGIN** | 📅 **SAMPLED** |

## SERVING TYPE

| CAN | BOTTLE | CASK | DRAFT | GROWLER | MIXED | OTHER |
|---|---|---|---|---|---|---|
| 🥫 | 🍾 | 🛢 | 🍺 | 🥛 | 🍹 | ⚗ |
| ☐ | ☐ | ☐ | ☐ | ☐ | ☐ | ☐ |

## BUBBLES & COLOR

HIGH ◯

SPARKLING ◯

MEDIUM ◯

STILL ◯

PALE AMBER ◯

MEDIUM AMBER ◯

DEEP AMBER ◯

AMBER BROWN ◯

BROWN ◯

ERUBY BROWN ◯

## FLAVOR WHEEL

CREAMY · SWEET · EARTHY · HERBAL · FLORAL · SPICY · BITTER · SOUR · HOPPY · MALTY · TOASTED · FRUITY · CARAMEL · COFFEE · NUTTY · DAIRY

## FINAL RATING

| | | |
|---|---|---|
| 🍾 APPEARANCE | ☆☆☆☆☆ |
| 🌾 AROMA | ☆☆☆☆☆ |
| 🍺 TASTE | ☆☆☆☆☆ |
| 👄 MOUTHFEEL | ☆☆☆☆☆ |
| 🤲 OVERALL RATING | ☆☆☆☆☆ |

## ADDITIONAL NOTES

## NAME

## BREWERY

## TYPE / STYLE

## ABV

## IBU

## ORIGIN

## SAMPLED

## SERVING TYPE

| CAN | BOTTLE | CASK | DRAFT | GROWLER | MIXED | OTHER |
|-----|--------|------|-------|---------|-------|-------|
| ☐ | ☐ | ☐ | ☐ | ☐ | ☐ | ☐ |

## BUBBLES & COLOR

HIGH

SPARKLING

MEDIUM

STILL

PALE AMBER

MEDIUM AMBER

DEEP AMBER

AMBER BROWN

BROWN

ERUBY BROWN

## FLAVOR WHEEL

CREAMY · SWEET · EARTHY · HERBAL · FLORAL · SPICY · BITTER · SOUR · HOPPY · MALTY · TOASTED · FRUITY · CARAMEL · COFFEE · NUTTY · DAIRY

## FINAL RATING

APPEARANCE ☆☆☆☆☆

AROMA ☆☆☆☆☆

TASTE ☆☆☆☆☆

MOUTHFEEL ☆☆☆☆☆

OVERALL RATING ☆☆☆☆☆

## ADDITIONAL NOTES

## NAME

| BREWERY | TYPE / STYLE |
|---|---|
| ABV | IBU |
| ORIGIN | SAMPLED |

## SERVING TYPE

| CAN | BOTTLE | CASK | DRAFT | GROWLER | MIXED | OTHER |
|---|---|---|---|---|---|---|
| ☐ | ☐ | ☐ | ☐ | ☐ | ☐ | ☐ |

## BUBBLES & COLOR

HIGH ○

SPARKLING ○

MEDIUM ○

STILL ○

PALE AMBER ○

MEDIUM AMBER ○

DEEP AMBER ○

AMBER BROWN ○

BROWN ○

ERUBY BROWN ○

## FLAVOR WHEEL

CREAMY SWEET EARTHY HERBAL
DAIRY FLORAL
NUTTY SPICY
COFFEE BITTER
CARAMEL SOUR
FRUITY TOASTED MALTY HOPPY

## FINAL RATING

| APPEARANCE | ☆☆☆☆☆ |
|---|---|
| AROMA | ☆☆☆☆☆ |
| TASTE | ☆☆☆☆☆ |
| MOUTHFEEL | ☆☆☆☆☆ |
| OVERALL RATING | ☆☆☆☆☆ |

## ADDITIONAL NOTES

## NAME

| | | | |
|---|---|---|---|
| **BREWERY** | | **TYPE / STYLE** | |
| **ABV** | | **IBU** | |
| **ORIGIN** | | **SAMPLED** | |

## SERVING TYPE

| CAN | BOTTLE | CASK | DRAFT | GROWLER | MIXED | OTHER |
|---|---|---|---|---|---|---|
| ☐ | ☐ | ☐ | ☐ | ☐ | ☐ | ☐ |

## BUBBLES & COLOR

HIGH

SPARKLING

MEDIUM

STILL

PALE AMBER

MEDIUM AMBER

DEEP AMBER

AMBER BROWN

BROWN

ERUBY BROWN

## FLAVOR WHEEL

CREAMY · SWEET · EARTHY · HERBAL · FLORAL · SPICY · BITTER · SOUR · HOPPY · MALTY · TOASTED · FRUITY · CARAMEL · COFFEE · NUTTY · DAIRY

## FINAL RATING

| APPEARANCE | ☆☆☆☆☆ |
|---|---|
| AROMA | ☆☆☆☆☆ |
| TASTE | ☆☆☆☆☆ |
| MOUTHFEEL | ☆☆☆☆☆ |
| OVERALL RATING | ☆☆☆☆☆ |

## ADDITIONAL NOTES

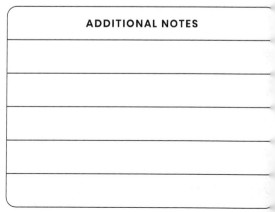

## NAME

| BREWERY | TYPE / STYLE |
|---|---|
| ABV | IBU |
| ORIGIN | SAMPLED |

## SERVING TYPE

| CAN | BOTTLE | CASK | DRAFT | GROWLER | MIXED | OTHER |
|---|---|---|---|---|---|---|
| ☐ | ☐ | ☐ | ☐ | ☐ | ☐ | ☐ |

## BUBBLES & COLOR

HIGH

SPARKLING

MEDIUM

STILL

PALE AMBER

MEDIUM AMBER

DEEP AMBER

AMBER BROWN

BROWN

ERUBY BROWN

## FLAVOR WHEEL

CREAMY · SWEET · EARTHY · HERBAL · FLORAL · SPICY · BITTER · SOUR · HOPPY · MALTY · TOASTED · FRUITY · CARAMEL · COFFEE · NUTTY · DAIRY

## FINAL RATING

| APPEARANCE | ☆☆☆☆☆ |
|---|---|
| AROMA | ☆☆☆☆☆ |
| TASTE | ☆☆☆☆☆ |
| MOUTHFEEL | ☆☆☆☆☆ |
| OVERALL RATING | ☆☆☆☆☆ |

## ADDITIONAL NOTES

## NAME

| BREWERY | TYPE / STYLE |
|---|---|
| ABV | IBU |
| ORIGIN | SAMPLED |

## SERVING TYPE

| CAN | BOTTLE | CASK | DRAFT | GROWLER | MIXED | OTHER |
|---|---|---|---|---|---|---|
| ☐ | ☐ | ☐ | ☐ | ☐ | ☐ | ☐ |

## BUBBLES & COLOR

HIGH

SPARKLING

MEDIUM

STILL

PALE AMBER
MEDIUM AMBER
DEEP AMBER
AMBER BROWN
BROWN
ERUBY BROWN

## FLAVOR WHEEL

CREAMY · SWEET · EARTHY · HERBAL · FLORAL · SPICY · BITTER · SOUR · HOPPY · MALTY · TOASTED · FRUITY · CARAMEL · COFFEE · NUTTY · DAIRY

## FINAL RATING

APPEARANCE ☆☆☆☆☆

AROMA ☆☆☆☆☆

TASTE ☆☆☆☆☆

MOUTHFEEL ☆☆☆☆☆

OVERALL RATING ☆☆☆☆☆

## ADDITIONAL NOTES

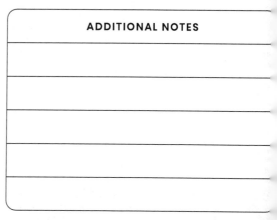

## NAME

| | |
|---|---|
| **BREWERY** | **TYPE / STYLE** |
| **ABV** | **IBU** |
| **ORIGIN** | **SAMPLED** |

## SERVING TYPE

| CAN | BOTTLE | CASK | DRAFT | GROWLER | MIXED | OTHER |
|---|---|---|---|---|---|---|
| ☐ | ☐ | ☐ | ☐ | ☐ | ☐ | ☐ |

## BUBBLES & COLOR

HIGH

SPARKLING

MEDIUM

STILL

PALE AMBER

MEDIUM AMBER

DEEP AMBER

AMBER BROWN

BROWN

ERUBY BROWN

## FLAVOR WHEEL

CREAMY · SWEET · EARTHY · HERBAL · FLORAL · SPICY · BITTER · SOUR · HOPPY · MALTY · TOASTED · FRUITY · CARAMEL · COFFEE · NUTTY · DAIRY

## FINAL RATING

| | | |
|---|---|---|
| APPEARANCE | ☆☆☆☆☆ |
| AROMA | ☆☆☆☆☆ |
| TASTE | ☆☆☆☆☆ |
| MOUTHFEEL | ☆☆☆☆☆ |
| OVERALL RATING | ☆☆☆☆☆ |

## ADDITIONAL NOTES

## NAME

| BREWERY | TYPE / STYLE |
|---|---|
| ABV | IBU |
| ORIGIN | SAMPLED |

## SERVING TYPE

| CAN | BOTTLE | CASK | DRAFT | GROWLER | MIXED | OTHER |
|---|---|---|---|---|---|---|
| ☐ | ☐ | ☐ | ☐ | ☐ | ☐ | ☐ |

## BUBBLES & COLOR

HIGH

SPARKLING

MEDIUM

STILL

PALE AMBER
MEDIUM AMBER
DEEP AMBER
AMBER BROWN
BROWN
ERUBY BROWN

## FLAVOR WHEEL

CREAMY · SWEET · EARTHY · HERBAL · FLORAL · SPICY · BITTER · SOUR · HOPPY · MALTY · TOASTED · FRUITY · CARAMEL · COFFEE · NUTTY · DAIRY

## FINAL RATING

| APPEARANCE | ☆☆☆☆☆ |
|---|---|
| AROMA | ☆☆☆☆☆ |
| TASTE | ☆☆☆☆☆ |
| MOUTHFEEL | ☆☆☆☆☆ |
| OVERALL RATING | ☆☆☆☆☆ |

## ADDITIONAL NOTES

## NAME

| BREWERY | TYPE / STYLE |
|---|---|
| ABV | IBU |
| ORIGIN | SAMPLED |

## SERVING TYPE

| CAN | BOTTLE | CASK | DRAFT | GROWLER | MIXED | OTHER |
|---|---|---|---|---|---|---|
| ☐ | ☐ | ☐ | ☐ | ☐ | ☐ | ☐ |

## BUBBLES & COLOR

HIGH

SPARKLING

MEDIUM

STILL

PALE AMBER
MEDIUM AMBER
DEEP AMBER
AMBER BROWN
BROWN
ERUBY BROWN

## FLAVOR WHEEL

CREAMY · SWEET · EARTHY · HERBAL · FLORAL · SPICY · BITTER · SOUR · HOPPY · MALTY · TOASTED · FRUITY · CARAMEL · COFFEE · NUTTY · DAIRY

## FINAL RATING

| APPEARANCE | ☆☆☆☆☆ |
|---|---|
| AROMA | ☆☆☆☆☆ |
| TASTE | ☆☆☆☆☆ |
| MOUTHFEEL | ☆☆☆☆☆ |
| OVERALL RATING | ☆☆☆☆☆ |

## ADDITIONAL NOTES

## NAME

| BREWERY | TYPE / STYLE |
|---|---|
| ABV | IBU |
| ORIGIN | SAMPLED |

## SERVING TYPE

| CAN | BOTTLE | CASK | DRAFT | GROWLER | MIXED | OTHER |
|---|---|---|---|---|---|---|
| ☐ | ☐ | ☐ | ☐ | ☐ | ☐ | ☐ |

## BUBBLES & COLOR

HIGH

SPARKLING

MEDIUM

STILL

PALE AMBER

MEDIUM AMBER

DEEP AMBER

AMBER BROWN

BROWN

ERUBY BROWN

## FLAVOR WHEEL

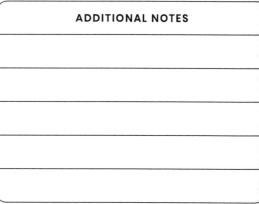

CREAMY · SWEET · EARTHY · HERBAL · FLORAL · SPICY · BITTER · SOUR · HOPPY · MALTY · TOASTED · FRUITY · CARAMEL · COFFEE · NUTTY · DAIRY

## FINAL RATING

| | | |
|---|---|---|
| APPEARANCE | ☆☆☆☆☆ | |
| AROMA | ☆☆☆☆☆ | |
| TASTE | ☆☆☆☆☆ | |
| MOUTHFEEL | ☆☆☆☆☆ | |
| OVERALL RATING | ☆☆☆☆☆ | |

## ADDITIONAL NOTES

## NAME

## BREWERY

## TYPE / STYLE

## ABV

## IBU

## ORIGIN

## SAMPLED

## SERVING TYPE

| CAN | BOTTLE | CASK | DRAFT | GROWLER | MIXED | OTHER |
|-----|--------|------|-------|---------|-------|-------|
| ☐ | ☐ | ☐ | ☐ | ☐ | ☐ | ☐ |

## BUBBLES & COLOR

HIGH ○

SPARKLING ○

MEDIUM ○

STILL ○

PALE AMBER ○

MEDIUM AMBER ○

DEEP AMBER ○

AMBER BROWN ○

BROWN ○

ERUBY BROWN ○

## FLAVOR WHEEL

CREAMY • SWEET • EARTHY • HERBAL • FLORAL • SPICY • BITTER • SOUR • HOPPY • MALTY • TOASTED • FRUITY • CARAMEL • COFFEE • NUTTY • DAIRY

## FINAL RATING

APPEARANCE ☆☆☆☆☆

AROMA ☆☆☆☆☆

TASTE ☆☆☆☆☆

MOUTHFEEL ☆☆☆☆☆

OVERALL RATING ☆☆☆☆☆

## ADDITIONAL NOTES

## NAME

| BREWERY | TYPE / STYLE |
|---|---|
| ABV | IBU |
| ORIGIN | SAMPLED |

## SERVING TYPE

| CAN | BOTTLE | CASK | DRAFT | GROWLER | MIXED | OTHER |
|---|---|---|---|---|---|---|
| ☐ | ☐ | ☐ | ☐ | ☐ | ☐ | ☐ |

## BUBBLES & COLOR

HIGH

SPARKLING

MEDIUM

STILL

PALE AMBER

MEDIUM AMBER

DEEP AMBER

AMBER BROWN

BROWN

ERUBY BROWN

## FLAVOR WHEEL

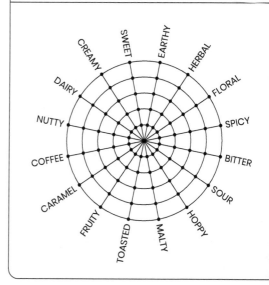

CREAMY · SWEET · EARTHY · HERBAL · FLORAL · SPICY · BITTER · SOUR · HOPPY · MALTY · TOASTED · FRUITY · CARAMEL · COFFEE · NUTTY · DAIRY

## FINAL RATING

| APPEARANCE | ☆☆☆☆☆ |
|---|---|
| AROMA | ☆☆☆☆☆ |
| TASTE | ☆☆☆☆☆ |
| MOUTHFEEL | ☆☆☆☆☆ |
| OVERALL RATING | ☆☆☆☆☆ |

## ADDITIONAL NOTES

## NAME

| | |
|---|---|
| BREWERY | TYPE / STYLE |
| ABV | IBU |
| ORIGIN | SAMPLED |

## SERVING TYPE

| CAN | BOTTLE | CASK | DRAFT | GROWLER | MIXED | OTHER |
|---|---|---|---|---|---|---|
| ☐ | ☐ | ☐ | ☐ | ☐ | ☐ | ☐ |

## BUBBLES & COLOR

HIGH

SPARKLING

MEDIUM

STILL

PALE AMBER
MEDIUM AMBER
DEEP AMBER
AMBER BROWN
BROWN
ERUBY BROWN

## FLAVOR WHEEL

CREAMY SWEET EARTHY HERBAL
DAIRY FLORAL
NUTTY SPICY
COFFEE BITTER
CARAMEL SOUR
FRUITY HOPPY
TOASTED MALTY

## FINAL RATING

| APPEARANCE | ☆☆☆☆☆ |
|---|---|
| AROMA | ☆☆☆☆☆ |
| TASTE | ☆☆☆☆☆ |
| MOUTHFEEL | ☆☆☆☆☆ |
| OVERALL RATING | ☆☆☆☆☆ |

## ADDITIONAL NOTES

## NAME

| 🍺 BREWERY | 🍶 TYPE / STYLE |
|---|---|
| 🍾 ABV | 🌿 IBU |
| 🌍 ORIGIN | 📅 SAMPLED |

## SERVING TYPE

| CAN | BOTTLE | CASK | DRAFT | GROWLER | MIXED | OTHER |
|---|---|---|---|---|---|---|
| ☐ | ☐ | ☐ | ☐ | ☐ | ☐ | ☐ |

## BUBBLES & COLOR

HIGH

SPARKLING

MEDIUM

STILL

PALE AMBER
MEDIUM AMBER
DEEP AMBER
AMBER BROWN
BROWN
ERUBY BROWN

## FLAVOR WHEEL

CREAMY · SWEET · EARTHY · HERBAL · FLORAL · SPICY · BITTER · SOUR · HOPPY · MALTY · TOASTED · FRUITY · CARAMEL · COFFEE · NUTTY · DAIRY

## FINAL RATING

| 🍾 APPEARANCE | ☆☆☆☆☆ |
|---|---|
| 🌾 AROMA | ☆☆☆☆☆ |
| 🍺 TASTE | ☆☆☆☆☆ |
| 👄 MOUTHFEEL | ☆☆☆☆☆ |
| 🤲 OVERALL RATING | ☆☆☆☆☆ |

## ADDITIONAL NOTES

## NAME

| BREWERY | TYPE / STYLE |
|---|---|
| ABV | IBU |
| ORIGIN | SAMPLED |

## SERVING TYPE

| CAN | BOTTLE | CASK | DRAFT | GROWLER | MIXED | OTHER |
|---|---|---|---|---|---|---|
| ☐ | ☐ | ☐ | ☐ | ☐ | ☐ | ☐ |

## BUBBLES & COLOR

HIGH ○

SPARKLING ○

MEDIUM ○

STILL ○

PALE AMBER ○

MEDIUM AMBER ○

DEEP AMBER ○

AMBER BROWN ○

BROWN ○

ERUBY BROWN ○

## FLAVOR WHEEL

CREAMY — SWEET — EARTHY — HERBAL — FLORAL — SPICY — BITTER — SOUR — HOPPY — MALTY — TOASTED — FRUITY — CARAMEL — COFFEE — NUTTY — DAIRY

## FINAL RATING

| APPEARANCE | ☆☆☆☆☆ |
|---|---|
| AROMA | ☆☆☆☆☆ |
| TASTE | ☆☆☆☆☆ |
| MOUTHFEEL | ☆☆☆☆☆ |
| OVERALL RATING | ☆☆☆☆☆ |

## ADDITIONAL NOTES

## NAME

| | |
|---|---|
| **BREWERY** | **TYPE / STYLE** |
| **ABV** | **IBU** |
| **ORIGIN** | **SAMPLED** |

## SERVING TYPE

| CAN | BOTTLE | CASK | DRAFT | GROWLER | MIXED | OTHER |
|---|---|---|---|---|---|---|
| ☐ | ☐ | ☐ | ☐ | ☐ | ☐ | ☐ |

## BUBBLES & COLOR

HIGH

SPARKLING

MEDIUM

STILL

PALE AMBER

MEDIUM AMBER

DEEP AMBER

AMBER BROWN

BROWN

ERUBY BROWN

## FLAVOR WHEEL

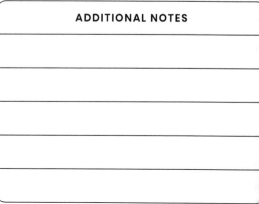

CREAMY · SWEET · EARTHY · HERBAL · FLORAL · SPICY · BITTER · SOUR · HOPPY · MALTY · TOASTED · FRUITY · CARAMEL · COFFEE · NUTTY · DAIRY

## FINAL RATING

| | |
|---|---|
| APPEARANCE | ☆☆☆☆☆ |
| AROMA | ☆☆☆☆☆ |
| TASTE | ☆☆☆☆☆ |
| MOUTHFEEL | ☆☆☆☆☆ |
| OVERALL RATING | ☆☆☆☆☆ |

## ADDITIONAL NOTES

## NAME

| BREWERY | TYPE / STYLE |
|---|---|
| ABV | IBU |
| ORIGIN | SAMPLED |

## SERVING TYPE

| CAN | BOTTLE | CASK | DRAFT | GROWLER | MIXED | OTHER |
|---|---|---|---|---|---|---|
| ☐ | ☐ | ☐ | ☐ | ☐ | ☐ | ☐ |

## BUBBLES & COLOR

HIGH

SPARKLING

MEDIUM

STILL

PALE AMBER

MEDIUM AMBER

DEEP AMBER

AMBER BROWN

BROWN

ERUBY BROWN

## FLAVOR WHEEL

CREAMY · SWEET · EARTHY · HERBAL · FLORAL · SPICY · BITTER · SOUR · HOPPY · MALTY · TOASTED · FRUITY · CARAMEL · COFFEE · NUTTY · DAIRY

## FINAL RATING

| APPEARANCE | ☆☆☆☆☆ |
|---|---|
| AROMA | ☆☆☆☆☆ |
| TASTE | ☆☆☆☆☆ |
| MOUTHFEEL | ☆☆☆☆☆ |
| OVERALL RATING | ☆☆☆☆☆ |

## ADDITIONAL NOTES

## NAME

| BREWERY | TYPE / STYLE |
|---|---|
| ABV | IBU |
| ORIGIN | SAMPLED |

## SERVING TYPE

| CAN | BOTTLE | CASK | DRAFT | GROWLER | MIXED | OTHER |
|---|---|---|---|---|---|---|
| ☐ | ☐ | ☐ | ☐ | ☐ | ☐ | ☐ |

## BUBBLES & COLOR

HIGH

SPARKLING

MEDIUM

STILL

PALE AMBER
MEDIUM AMBER
DEEP AMBER
AMBER BROWN
BROWN
ERUBY BROWN

## FLAVOR WHEEL

CREAMY · SWEET · EARTHY · HERBAL · FLORAL · SPICY · BITTER · SOUR · HOPPY · MALTY · TOASTED · FRUITY · CARAMEL · COFFEE · NUTTY · DAIRY

## FINAL RATING

| APPEARANCE | ☆☆☆☆☆ |
|---|---|
| AROMA | ☆☆☆☆☆ |
| TASTE | ☆☆☆☆☆ |
| MOUTHFEEL | ☆☆☆☆☆ |
| OVERALL RATING | ☆☆☆☆☆ |

## ADDITIONAL NOTES

## NAME

| BREWERY | TYPE / STYLE |
|---|---|
| ABV | IBU |
| ORIGIN | SAMPLED |

## SERVING TYPE

| CAN | BOTTLE | CASK | DRAFT | GROWLER | MIXED | OTHER |
|---|---|---|---|---|---|---|
| ☐ | ☐ | ☐ | ☐ | ☐ | ☐ | ☐ |

## BUBBLES & COLOR

HIGH

SPARKLING

MEDIUM

STILL

PALE AMBER ☐
MEDIUM AMBER ☐
DEEP AMBER ☐
AMBER BROWN ☐
BROWN ☐
ERUBY BROWN ☐

## FLAVOR WHEEL

CREAMY — SWEET — EARTHY — HERBAL — FLORAL — SPICY — BITTER — SOUR — HOPPY — MALTY — TOASTED — FRUITY — CARAMEL — COFFEE — NUTTY — DAIRY

## FINAL RATING

| APPEARANCE | ☆☆☆☆☆ |
|---|---|
| AROMA | ☆☆☆☆☆ |
| TASTE | ☆☆☆☆☆ |
| MOUTHFEEL | ☆☆☆☆☆ |
| OVERALL RATING | ☆☆☆☆☆ |

## ADDITIONAL NOTES

## NAME

## BREWERY

## TYPE / STYLE

## ABV

## IBU

## ORIGIN

## SAMPLED

## SERVING TYPE

| CAN | BOTTLE | CASK | DRAFT | GROWLER | MIXED | OTHER |
|-----|--------|------|-------|---------|-------|-------|
| ☐ | ☐ | ☐ | ☐ | ☐ | ☐ | ☐ |

## BUBBLES & COLOR

HIGH

SPARKLING

MEDIUM

STILL

PALE AMBER

MEDIUM AMBER

DEEP AMBER

AMBER BROWN

BROWN

ERUBY BROWN

## FLAVOR WHEEL

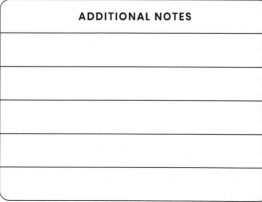

CREAMY
SWEET
EARTHY
HERBAL
DAIRY
FLORAL
NUTTY
SPICY
COFFEE
BITTER
CARAMEL
SOUR
FRUITY
HOPPY
TOASTED
MALTY

## FINAL RATING

| | | |
|---|---|---|
| APPEARANCE | ☆☆☆☆☆ |
| AROMA | ☆☆☆☆☆ |
| TASTE | ☆☆☆☆☆ |
| MOUTHFEEL | ☆☆☆☆☆ |
| OVERALL RATING | ☆☆☆☆☆ |

## ADDITIONAL NOTES

| 🍺 NAME | |
|---|---|
| 🛢️ BREWERY | 🍾 TYPE / STYLE |
| 🍶 ABV | 🌿 IBU |
| 🌍 ORIGIN | 📅 SAMPLED |

## SERVING TYPE

| CAN | BOTTLE | CASK | DRAFT | GROWLER | MIXED | OTHER |
|---|---|---|---|---|---|---|
| 🧃 | 🍾 | 🛢️ | 🍺 | 🫙 | 🍹 | ⚗️ |
| ☐ | ☐ | ☐ | ☐ | ☐ | ☐ | ☐ |

## BUBBLES & COLOR

| | | |
|---|---|---|
| HIGH | PALE AMBER | ◯ |
| | MEDIUM AMBER | ◯ |
| SPARKLING | DEEP AMBER | ◯ |
| | AMBER BROWN | ◯ |
| MEDIUM | BROWN | ◯ |
| STILL | ERUBY BROWN | ◯ |

## FLAVOR WHEEL

CREAMY · SWEET · EARTHY · HERBAL · FLORAL · SPICY · BITTER · SOUR · HOPPY · MALTY · TOASTED · FRUITY · CARAMEL · COFFEE · NUTTY · DAIRY

## FINAL RATING

| | | |
|---|---|---|
| 🍾 APPEARANCE | ☆☆☆☆☆ |
| 🌾 AROMA | ☆☆☆☆☆ |
| 🍺 TASTE | ☆☆☆☆☆ |
| 🍫 MOUTHFEEL | ☆☆☆☆☆ |
| 🖐️ OVERALL RATING | ☆☆☆☆☆ |

## ADDITIONAL NOTES

| 🍺 NAME | |
|---|---|
| 🛢 BREWERY | 🏺 TYPE / STYLE |
| 🍶 ABV | 🌿 IBU |
| 🌍 ORIGIN | 📅 SAMPLED |

## SERVING TYPE

| CAN | BOTTLE | CASK | DRAFT | GROWLER | MIXED | OTHER |
|---|---|---|---|---|---|---|
| ☐ | ☐ | ☐ | ☐ | ☐ | ☐ | ☐ |

## BUBBLES & COLOR

HIGH

SPARKLING

MEDIUM

STILL

PALE AMBER
MEDIUM AMBER
DEEP AMBER
AMBER BROWN
BROWN
ERUBY BROWN

## FLAVOR WHEEL

CREAMY · SWEET · EARTHY · HERBAL · FLORAL · SPICY · BITTER · SOUR · HOPPY · MALTY · TOASTED · FRUITY · CARAMEL · COFFEE · NUTTY · DAIRY

## FINAL RATING

| 🍾 APPEARANCE | ☆☆☆☆☆ |
|---|---|
| 🌾 AROMA | ☆☆☆☆☆ |
| 🍺 TASTE | ☆☆☆☆☆ |
| 👄 MOUTHFEEL | ☆☆☆☆☆ |
| ⭐ OVERALL RATING | ☆☆☆☆☆ |

## ADDITIONAL NOTES

## NAME

| BREWERY | TYPE / STYLE |
|---|---|
| ABV | IBU |
| ORIGIN | SAMPLED |

## SERVING TYPE

| CAN | BOTTLE | CASK | DRAFT | GROWLER | MIXED | OTHER |
|---|---|---|---|---|---|---|
| ☐ | ☐ | ☐ | ☐ | ☐ | ☐ | ☐ |

## BUBBLES & COLOR

HIGH

SPARKLING

MEDIUM

STILL

PALE AMBER

MEDIUM AMBER

DEEP AMBER

AMBER BROWN

BROWN

ERUBY BROWN

## FLAVOR WHEEL

CREAMY · SWEET · EARTHY · HERBAL · FLORAL · SPICY · BITTER · SOUR · HOPPY · MALTY · TOASTED · FRUITY · CARAMEL · COFFEE · NUTTY · DAIRY

## FINAL RATING

| APPEARANCE | ☆☆☆☆☆ |
|---|---|
| AROMA | ☆☆☆☆☆ |
| TASTE | ☆☆☆☆☆ |
| MOUTHFEEL | ☆☆☆☆☆ |
| OVERALL RATING | ☆☆☆☆☆ |

## ADDITIONAL NOTES

## NAME

| BREWERY | TYPE / STYLE |
|---|---|
| ABV | IBU |
| ORIGIN | SAMPLED |

## SERVING TYPE

| CAN | BOTTLE | CASK | DRAFT | GROWLER | MIXED | OTHER |
|---|---|---|---|---|---|---|
| ☐ | ☐ | ☐ | ☐ | ☐ | ☐ | ☐ |

## BUBBLES & COLOR

HIGH

SPARKLING

MEDIUM

STILL

PALE AMBER

MEDIUM AMBER

DEEP AMBER

AMBER BROWN

BROWN

ERUBY BROWN

## FLAVOR WHEEL

CREAMY · SWEET · EARTHY · HERBAL · FLORAL · DAIRY · SPICY · NUTTY · BITTER · COFFEE · SOUR · CARAMEL · HOPPY · FRUITY · MALTY · TOASTED

## FINAL RATING

| APPEARANCE | ☆☆☆☆☆ |
|---|---|
| AROMA | ☆☆☆☆☆ |
| TASTE | ☆☆☆☆☆ |
| MOUTHFEEL | ☆☆☆☆☆ |
| OVERALL RATING | ☆☆☆☆☆ |

## ADDITIONAL NOTES

## NAME

| BREWERY | TYPE / STYLE |
|---|---|
| ABV | IBU |
| ORIGIN | SAMPLED |

## SERVING TYPE

| CAN | BOTTLE | CASK | DRAFT | GROWLER | MIXED | OTHER |
|---|---|---|---|---|---|---|
| ☐ | ☐ | ☐ | ☐ | ☐ | ☐ | ☐ |

## BUBBLES & COLOR

HIGH ○

SPARKLING ○

MEDIUM ○

STILL ○

PALE AMBER ○

MEDIUM AMBER ○

DEEP AMBER ○

AMBER BROWN ○

BROWN ○

ERUBY BROWN ○

## FLAVOR WHEEL

CREAMY · SWEET · EARTHY · HERBAL · FLORAL · SPICY · BITTER · SOUR · HOPPY · MALTY · TOASTED · FRUITY · CARAMEL · COFFEE · NUTTY · DAIRY

## FINAL RATING

| APPEARANCE | ☆☆☆☆☆ |
|---|---|
| AROMA | ☆☆☆☆☆ |
| TASTE | ☆☆☆☆☆ |
| MOUTHFEEL | ☆☆☆☆☆ |
| OVERALL RATING | ☆☆☆☆☆ |

## ADDITIONAL NOTES

| 🍺 NAME | |
|---|---|
| 🛢 BREWERY | 🍾 TYPE / STYLE |
| 🍶 ABV | 🌿 IBU |
| 🌎 ORIGIN | 📅 SAMPLED |

## SERVING TYPE

| CAN | BOTTLE | CASK | DRAFT | GROWLER | MIXED | OTHER |
|---|---|---|---|---|---|---|
| 🥫 | 🍾 | 🛢 | 🍺 | 🧃 | 🍹 | 🧪 |
| ☐ | ☐ | ☐ | ☐ | ☐ | ☐ | ☐ |

## BUBBLES & COLOR

HIGH

SPARKLING

MEDIUM

STILL

PALE AMBER

MEDIUM AMBER

DEEP AMBER

AMBER BROWN

BROWN

ERUBY BROWN

## FLAVOR WHEEL

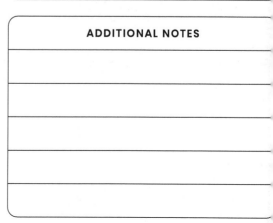

CREAMY · SWEET · EARTHY · HERBAL · DAIRY · FLORAL · NUTTY · SPICY · COFFEE · BITTER · CARAMEL · SOUR · FRUITY · HOPPY · TOASTED · MALTY

## FINAL RATING

| | | |
|---|---|---|
| 🍾 APPEARANCE | ☆☆☆☆☆ |
| 🌾 AROMA | ☆☆☆☆☆ |
| 🍺 TASTE | ☆☆☆☆☆ |
| 👄 MOUTHFEEL | ☆☆☆☆☆ |
| 🖐 OVERALL RATING | ☆☆☆☆☆ |

## ADDITIONAL NOTES

| 🍺 NAME | | |
|---|---|---|
| 🛢 BREWERY | | 🍾 TYPE / STYLE |
| 🍶 ABV | | 🌿 IBU |
| 🌍 ORIGIN | | 📅 SAMPLED |

## SERVING TYPE

| CAN | BOTTLE | CASK | DRAFT | GROWLER | MIXED | OTHER |
|---|---|---|---|---|---|---|
| 🥫 | 🍾 | 🛢 | 🍺 | 🧃 | 🍹 | ⚗ |
| ☐ | ☐ | ☐ | ☐ | ☐ | ☐ | ☐ |

## BUBBLES & COLOR

HIGH ○

SPARKLING ○

MEDIUM ○

STILL ○

PALE AMBER ○

MEDIUM AMBER ○

DEEP AMBER ○

AMBER BROWN ○

BROWN ○

ERUBY BROWN ○

## FLAVOR WHEEL

CREAMY · SWEET · EARTHY · HERBAL · FLORAL · SPICY · BITTER · SOUR · HOPPY · MALTY · TOASTED · FRUITY · CARAMEL · COFFEE · NUTTY · DAIRY

## FINAL RATING

| 🍾 APPEARANCE | ☆☆☆☆☆ |
|---|---|
| 🌾 AROMA | ☆☆☆☆☆ |
| 🍺 TASTE | ☆☆☆☆☆ |
| 👄 MOUTHFEEL | ☆☆☆☆☆ |
| 🤲 OVERALL RATING | ☆☆☆☆☆ |

## ADDITIONAL NOTES

| 🍺 NAME | |
| --- | --- |
| 🛢 BREWERY | 🍾 TYPE / STYLE |
| 🍶 ABV | 🌿 IBU |
| 🌐 ORIGIN | 📅 SAMPLED |

## SERVING TYPE

| CAN | BOTTLE | CASK | DRAFT | GROWLER | MIXED | OTHER |
| --- | --- | --- | --- | --- | --- | --- |
| ☐ | ☐ | ☐ | ☐ | ☐ | ☐ | ☐ |

## BUBBLES & COLOR

HIGH

SPARKLING

MEDIUM

STILL

PALE AMBER

MEDIUM AMBER

DEEP AMBER

AMBER BROWN

BROWN

ERUBY BROWN

## FLAVOR WHEEL

CREAMY · SWEET · EARTHY · HERBAL · FLORAL · SPICY · BITTER · SOUR · HOPPY · MALTY · TOASTED · FRUITY · CARAMEL · COFFEE · NUTTY · DAIRY

## FINAL RATING

| 🍾 APPEARANCE | ☆☆☆☆☆ |
| --- | --- |
| 🌾 AROMA | ☆☆☆☆☆ |
| 🍺 TASTE | ☆☆☆☆☆ |
| 👄 MOUTHFEEL | ☆☆☆☆☆ |
| 🤲 OVERALL RATING | ☆☆☆☆☆ |

## ADDITIONAL NOTES

| 🍺 **NAME** | |
|---|---|
| 🛢 **BREWERY** | 🫙 **TYPE / STYLE** |
| 🍾 **ABV** | 🌰 **IBU** |
| 🌍 **ORIGIN** | 📅 **SAMPLED** |

## SERVING TYPE

| CAN | BOTTLE | CASK | DRAFT | GROWLER | MIXED | OTHER |
|---|---|---|---|---|---|---|
| ☐ | ☐ | ☐ | ☐ | ☐ | ☐ | ☐ |

## BUBBLES & COLOR

HIGH

SPARKLING

MEDIUM

STILL

- PALE AMBER ○
- MEDIUM AMBER ○
- DEEP AMBER ○
- AMBER BROWN ○
- BROWN ○
- ERUBY BROWN ○

## FLAVOR WHEEL

CREAMY · SWEET · EARTHY · HERBAL · FLORAL · SPICY · BITTER · SOUR · HOPPY · MALTY · TOASTED · FRUITY · CARAMEL · COFFEE · NUTTY · DAIRY

## FINAL RATING

| 🧴 APPEARANCE | ☆☆☆☆☆ |
|---|---|
| 🌾 AROMA | ☆☆☆☆☆ |
| 🍺 TASTE | ☆☆☆☆☆ |
| 👄 MOUTHFEEL | ☆☆☆☆☆ |
| 🤲 OVERALL RATING | ☆☆☆☆☆ |

## ADDITIONAL NOTES

| 🍺 NAME | |
|---|---|
| 🛢️ BREWERY | 🧪 TYPE / STYLE |
| 🍾 ABV | 🌿 IBU |
| 🌍 ORIGIN | 📅 SAMPLED |

## SERVING TYPE

| CAN | BOTTLE | CASK | DRAFT | GROWLER | MIXED | OTHER |
|---|---|---|---|---|---|---|
| 🥫 ☐ | 🍾 ☐ | 🛢️ ☐ | 🍺 ☐ | 🫗 ☐ | 🍹 ☐ | ⚗️ ☐ |

## BUBBLES & COLOR

HIGH ○

SPARKLING ○

MEDIUM ○

STILL ○

PALE AMBER ○

MEDIUM AMBER ○

DEEP AMBER ○

AMBER BROWN ○

BROWN ○

ERUBY BROWN ○

## FLAVOR WHEEL

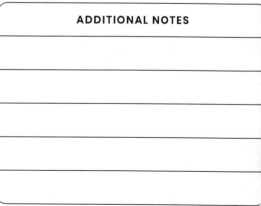

CREAMY · SWEET · EARTHY · HERBAL · FLORAL · SPICY · BITTER · SOUR · HOPPY · MALTY · TOASTED · FRUITY · CARAMEL · COFFEE · NUTTY · DAIRY

## FINAL RATING

| 🍾 APPEARANCE | ☆☆☆☆☆ |
|---|---|
| 🌾 AROMA | ☆☆☆☆☆ |
| 🍺 TASTE | ☆☆☆☆☆ |
| 👄 MOUTHFEEL | ☆☆☆☆☆ |
| 🤲 OVERALL RATING | ☆☆☆☆☆ |

## ADDITIONAL NOTES

## NAME

| BREWERY | TYPE / STYLE |
|---------|--------------|
| ABV | IBU |
| ORIGIN | SAMPLED |

## SERVING TYPE

| CAN | BOTTLE | CASK | DRAFT | GROWLER | MIXED | OTHER |
|-----|--------|------|-------|---------|-------|-------|
| ☐ | ☐ | ☐ | ☐ | ☐ | ☐ | ☐ |

## BUBBLES & COLOR

HIGH

SPARKLING

MEDIUM

STILL

PALE AMBER ○
MEDIUM AMBER ○
DEEP AMBER ○
AMBER BROWN ○
BROWN ○
ERUBY BROWN ○

## FLAVOR WHEEL

CREAMY  SWEET  EARTHY  HERBAL
DAIRY  FLORAL
NUTTY  SPICY
COFFEE  BITTER
CARAMEL  SOUR
FRUITY  TOASTED  MALTY  HOPPY

## FINAL RATING

| ☆ APPEARANCE | ☆☆☆☆☆ |
|--------------|--------|
| AROMA | ☆☆☆☆☆ |
| TASTE | ☆☆☆☆☆ |
| MOUTHFEEL | ☆☆☆☆☆ |
| OVERALL RATING | ☆☆☆☆☆ |

## ADDITIONAL NOTES

## NAME

## BREWERY

## TYPE / STYLE

## ABV

## IBU

## ORIGIN

## SAMPLED

## SERVING TYPE

| CAN | BOTTLE | CASK | DRAFT | GROWLER | MIXED | OTHER |
|-----|--------|------|-------|---------|-------|-------|
| ☐ | ☐ | ☐ | ☐ | ☐ | ☐ | ☐ |

## BUBBLES & COLOR

HIGH

SPARKLING

MEDIUM

STILL

PALE AMBER

MEDIUM AMBER

DEEP AMBER

AMBER BROWN

BROWN

ERUBY BROWN

## FLAVOR WHEEL

CREAMY · SWEET · EARTHY · HERBAL · FLORAL · SPICY · BITTER · SOUR · HOPPY · MALTY · TOASTED · FRUITY · CARAMEL · COFFEE · NUTTY · DAIRY

## FINAL RATING

APPEARANCE ☆☆☆☆☆

AROMA ☆☆☆☆☆

TASTE ☆☆☆☆☆

MOUTHFEEL ☆☆☆☆☆

OVERALL RATING ☆☆☆☆☆

## ADDITIONAL NOTES

## NAME

| BREWERY | TYPE / STYLE |
|---|---|
| ABV | IBU |
| ORIGIN | SAMPLED |

## SERVING TYPE

| CAN | BOTTLE | CASK | DRAFT | GROWLER | MIXED | OTHER |
|---|---|---|---|---|---|---|
| ☐ | ☐ | ☐ | ☐ | ☐ | ☐ | ☐ |

## BUBBLES & COLOR

HIGH

SPARKLING

MEDIUM

STILL

PALE AMBER

MEDIUM AMBER

DEEP AMBER

AMBER BROWN

BROWN

ERUBY BROWN

## FLAVOR WHEEL

CREAMY · SWEET · EARTHY · HERBAL · FLORAL · SPICY · BITTER · SOUR · HOPPY · MALTY · TOASTED · FRUITY · CARAMEL · COFFEE · NUTTY · DAIRY

## FINAL RATING

| APPEARANCE | ☆☆☆☆☆ |
|---|---|
| AROMA | ☆☆☆☆☆ |
| TASTE | ☆☆☆☆☆ |
| MOUTHFEEL | ☆☆☆☆☆ |
| OVERALL RATING | ☆☆☆☆☆ |

## ADDITIONAL NOTES

## NAME

## BREWERY

## TYPE / STYLE

## ABV

## IBU

## ORIGIN

## SAMPLED

## SERVING TYPE

| CAN | BOTTLE | CASK | DRAFT | GROWLER | MIXED | OTHER |
|-----|--------|------|-------|---------|-------|-------|
| ☐ | ☐ | ☐ | ☐ | ☐ | ☐ | ☐ |

## BUBBLES & COLOR

HIGH

SPARKLING

MEDIUM

STILL

PALE AMBER

MEDIUM AMBER

DEEP AMBER

AMBER BROWN

BROWN

ERUBY BROWN

## FLAVOR WHEEL

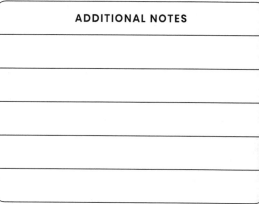

CREAMY · SWEET · EARTHY · HERBAL · FLORAL · SPICY · BITTER · SOUR · HOPPY · MALTY · TOASTED · FRUITY · CARAMEL · COFFEE · NUTTY · DAIRY

## FINAL RATING

| | | |
|---|---|---|
| APPEARANCE | ☆☆☆☆☆ | |
| AROMA | ☆☆☆☆☆ | |
| TASTE | ☆☆☆☆☆ | |
| MOUTHFEEL | ☆☆☆☆☆ | |
| OVERALL RATING | ☆☆☆☆☆ | |

## ADDITIONAL NOTES

## NAME

| BREWERY | TYPE / STYLE |
|---|---|
| ABV | IBU |
| ORIGIN | SAMPLED |

## SERVING TYPE

| CAN | BOTTLE | CASK | DRAFT | GROWLER | MIXED | OTHER |
|---|---|---|---|---|---|---|
| ☐ | ☐ | ☐ | ☐ | ☐ | ☐ | ☐ |

## BUBBLES & COLOR

HIGH

SPARKLING

MEDIUM

STILL

PALE AMBER

MEDIUM AMBER

DEEP AMBER

AMBER BROWN

BROWN

ERUBY BROWN

## FLAVOR WHEEL

CREAMY · SWEET · EARTHY · HERBAL · FLORAL · SPICY · BITTER · SOUR · HOPPY · MALTY · TOASTED · FRUITY · CARAMEL · COFFEE · NUTTY · DAIRY

## FINAL RATING

| APPEARANCE | ☆☆☆☆☆ |
|---|---|
| AROMA | ☆☆☆☆☆ |
| TASTE | ☆☆☆☆☆ |
| MOUTHFEEL | ☆☆☆☆☆ |
| OVERALL RATING | ☆☆☆☆☆ |

## ADDITIONAL NOTES

| 🍺 NAME | |
|---|---|
| 🛢️ BREWERY | 🧴 TYPE / STYLE |
| 🍾 ABV | 🌺 IBU |
| 🌐 ORIGIN | 📅 SAMPLED |

## SERVING TYPE

| CAN | BOTTLE | CASK | DRAFT | GROWLER | MIXED | OTHER |
|---|---|---|---|---|---|---|
| 🥫 | 🍾 | 🛢️ | 🍺 | 🫙 | 🍹 | ⚗️ |
| ☐ | ☐ | ☐ | ☐ | ☐ | ☐ | ☐ |

## BUBBLES & COLOR

HIGH

SPARKLING

MEDIUM

STILL

PALE AMBER ◯
MEDIUM AMBER ◯
DEEP AMBER ◯
AMBER BROWN ◯
BROWN ◯
ERUBY BROWN ◯

## FLAVOR WHEEL

CREAMY · SWEET · EARTHY · HERBAL · FLORAL · SPICY · BITTER · SOUR · HOPPY · MALTY · TOASTED · FRUITY · CARAMEL · COFFEE · NUTTY · DAIRY

## FINAL RATING

| 🍾 APPEARANCE | ☆☆☆☆☆ |
|---|---|
| 🌾 AROMA | ☆☆☆☆☆ |
| 🍺 TASTE | ☆☆☆☆☆ |
| 👄 MOUTHFEEL | ☆☆☆☆☆ |
| 🤲 OVERALL RATING | ☆☆☆☆☆ |

## ADDITIONAL NOTES

Made in the USA
Columbia, SC
09 October 2022

69195395R00062